The Darién Gap

The Darién Gap

A Reporter's Journey through the
Deadly Crossroads of the Americas

BELÉN FERNÁNDEZ

Rutgers University Press

New Brunswick, Camden, and Newark, New Jersey

London and Oxford

Rutgers University Press is a department of Rutgers, The State University of New Jersey, one of the leading public research universities in the nation. By publishing worldwide, it furthers the University's mission of dedication to excellence in teaching, scholarship, research, and clinical care.

Cataloging-in-publication data is available from the Library of Congress.
LCCN 2024050551

978-1-9788-4208-3 (cloth)
978-1-9788-4210-6 (epub)

A British Cataloging-in-Publication record for this book is available from the British Library.

References to internet websites (URLs) were accurate at the time of writing. Neither the author nor Rutgers University Press is responsible for URLs that may have expired or changed since the manuscript was prepared.

♾ The paper used in this publication meets the requirements of the American National Standard for Information Sciences—Permanence of Paper for Printed Library Materials, ANSI Z39.48-1992.

rutgersuniversitypress.org

For my dad

Contents

Introduction   1

The Darién Gap   9

Notes   185

Further Reading   193

The Darién Gap

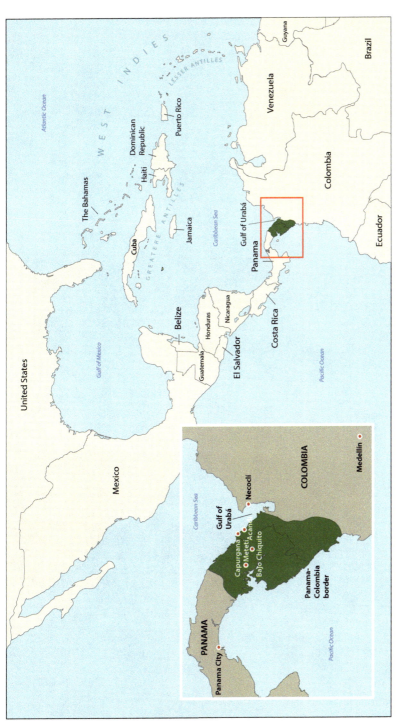

Darién Gap and Environs

Introduction

The first time I spoke with survivors of the Darién Gap, I was in jail in Mexico. It was July 2021, and I was serving a brief stint as the token gringa inmate in Mexico's largest immigration detention center, located in the city of Tapachula, Chiapas, just west of the border with Guatemala. Over 2,000 kilometers to the southeast of Tapachula lies the Darién Gap, known in Spanish as *el Tapón del Darién* or "the Darién Plug": the 106-kilometer stretch of territory that straddles Panama and Colombia and constitutes the only roadless interruption in the Pan-American Highway linking Alaska to the tip of Argentina. The Darién Gap encompasses a spectacularly hostile jungle that has in recent years become a mass migrant graveyard, as hundreds of thousands of refuge seekers from across the world are forced to contend with its horrors while pursuing the prospect of a better life in the United States, still some 5,000 kilometers away.[1]

The Tapachula jail was inaugurated with U.S. blessings in 2006 during the presidency of former Coca-Cola Mexico CEO Vicente Fox, whose administration had with either witting or unwitting irony bestowed the name "Siglo XXI" upon the facility, meaning "twenty-first century." Having overstayed my Mexican visa during the coronavirus pandemic in 2020 and then relied on the fake-Mexican-entry-form-mongering services of an immigration official in Mexico City, I was nabbed at Tapachula airport while attempting to board a domestic Mexican flight and hauled off to Siglo XXI for a twenty-four-hour glimpse of a twenty-first-century border apparatus designed to thwart the movement of U.S.-bound migrants.

Under normal circumstances, journalists are banned from entering the prison—and it's not hard to see why. The over-crowded, unhygienic conditions reek of human rights abuses, while the space resembles a psychological torture den for folks who have so often risked their lives to get this far and who are given no idea of when they might be released or deported. I met women who had already been held for a month or more and heard more than one detainee proclaim matter-of-factly: "I'm going to leave this place traumatized."

And it was within the walls of Siglo XXI that the Darién Gap entered my consciousness as something more than another nebu-lous epicenter of the global "migration crisis"—a crisis in which the United States forever portrays itself as being the foremost vic-tim despite perpetrating much of the international political and economic havoc that makes people migrate in the first place. It was not for no reason, after all, that Martin Luther King Jr. appointed the United States the "greatest purveyor of violence in the world," a distinction the country retains to this day.[2] My introduction to the jungle transpired on the cement sports court in the women's section of Siglo XXI, which with its single deflated ball represented the lone ostensible recreation option for inmates. I had no way of knowing at the start of my incarceration that my release would be so swift, having been assured otherwise by the carceral powers that be, and I had taken to plodding around the perimeter of the court in my sneakers—relieved of their shoelaces "for my security"—in an effort to ward off a nervous breakdown.

As happened at various times during my expedited twenty-first-century stopover, I was rescued from the perils of my own mind by my fellow detainees, who by and large charitably restricted their reactions to my nationality—and the presence of a U.S. citi-zen in a Mexican migrant jail—to hysterical laughter. Although perplexed by my deathly fear of being deported to the very country they were risking death to reach, a homeland I had spent the past eighteen years avoiding thanks to the international freedom of movement conferred by my U.S. passport, my prison mates offered nothing but solidarity in the face of made-in-USA structural inhumanity. I had clocked no more than a few minutes of martyrial plodding before I was wrested from the impending psychological abyss by a group of migrants seated on the ground nearby, who amiably commanded me to cease my solitude and sit with them.

The group comprised women from Cuba, El Salvador, Honduras, Nicaragua, and Venezuela, all nations with rather extensive histories on the receiving end of nefarious imperial meddling and even "large-scale terrorist war," as Noam Chomsky has described U.S.-backed Contra activities in Central America in the 1980s. One of the Hondurans, a bespectacled twenty-year-old university student fleeing the homicidal shit show in her country—which had only gotten worse in the aftermath of the 2009 U.S.-facilitated coup d'état against the democratically elected president, Manuel Zelaya—would subsequently hold up her towel for me in the curtainless bathrooms such that I would not have to bathe in full view of the uniformed Mexican immigration official who was supervising shower operations. For the moment, though, the student was lying on the ground with her head in a Cuban lap as the Cubans and Venezuelans in the group recounted stories from the Darién Gap, which geographical circumstances had spared the other present nationalities from having to traverse.

The Cubans did most of the storytelling. It had taken them one week to cross *la selva del Darién*, the Darién jungle, by the end of which time they had run out of food and water. They had navigated mountains of mud and rushing rivers and had witnessed some of their compatriots rescue a group of other migrants from near-certain death in a ravine, prompting the following satisfied analysis from one of the storytellers: "Say what you will about our manners, but at the end of the day *el hombre cubano* is very humanitarian."

The selva was strewn with corpses, the Cubans reported, which were in varying stages of decomposition and which served as further terrifying motivation to keep moving. They had personally known more than one individual who had gone into the jungle and never come out, and yet the most traumatizing component of the whole experience, it seemed, had involved a thirteen-year-old girl of unspecified nationality who had been raped repeatedly along the way. The girl's screams clearly continued to haunt the Cubans—and even more so now that they had been condemned to indefinite twenty-first-century limbo in Tapachula, where the traumatic trajectory had caught up to them. At least in the jungle, one of the women reasoned, you were focused on forward motion and didn't have much time to think.

For most of my own time in Siglo XXI I was deprived of a writing utensil, having had mine confiscated along with my shoelaces upon admittance to the facility. During one of the brief interludes when I was able to seize hold of the prison's only pen, which was attached to the wall and usually permanently tied up in detainee list-signing charades, I frantically scribbled some notes, including a line of Cuban jungle wisdom: "Cubans say no one leaves their country and walks thru selva for a week if they don't have to."

Although this sentiment naturally does not jibe with xenophobic fearmongering about malevolent migrant hordes bent on upending the world order and vanquishing the white race, it is at the end of the day a most accurate reflection of reality. And while migration has since the dawn of time been the most natural of phenomena, its current criminalization for the have-nots of the world helps sustain a lucrative global order predicated on the tyranny of capital and a hierarchy of human life.

My sole night in Siglo XXI was spent on half of the floor mat assigned to a young Cuban woman named Daniely, who insisted that I share it with her when the only available space for my own floor mat was abutting the toilet. Daniely also provided me with some spare clothes for use as a pillow, as well as an opinion on my decision to wear a coronavirus face mask: "Will you take that fucking thing off—I feel like I can't breathe."

To be sure, citizens of Cuba were well acquainted with asphyxiating situations; seven short months later, in February 2022, the United States' economic sanctions against the island would celebrate their sixtieth birthday. Following one very long night in July 2021, meanwhile, I was sprung from the suffocating confines of Siglo XXI thanks only to an intervention by a Mexican journalist friend of mine who pulled political strings at high levels. The U.S. embassy in Mexico City, for its part, had hung up on my mother after professionally inquiring whether I was a genuine U.S. citizen or just some naturalized María Belén Fernández.

Of course, whether or not the United States cared about me did not ultimately impact my imperial privilege, and rather than being justly punished for breaking Mexican immigration law, I was instead presented with a brand-new six-month entry permit for Mexico. Post-incarceration, I gradually resumed my pre-pandemic modus operandi of manic itinerance, dashing between countries like it was going out of style but now utilizing the coastal town of Zipolite in the Mexican state of Oaxaca as a semi-base. I flew to Turkey and Albania and returned to Zipolite; I flew to El Salvador and Suriname and returned again. I paid two more visits to Tapachula, both mercifully sans jail time, and two visits to Panama, all of which served to bring me into contact with more and more humans—from Venezuelans to Haitians to Afghans to Bangladeshis—who had seen no other option but to leave their countries and walk through the selva for a week.

In 2023 alone, more than 520,000 refuge seekers would survive the Darién Gap crossing, which was more than double the nearly 250,000 who crossed in 2022 and nearly four times the 133,000 who crossed in 2021. The drastic uptick was attributable to a combination of factors, including the disproportionate repercussions of the pandemic on the global poor and punitive visa restrictions leveled against Venezuelans in 2022 by Mexico, Costa Rica, and Belize, eliminating the possibility of air travel to those countries for many citizens of Venezuela and propelling them to the position of most represented nationality in the Gap. The number of migrants who have died trying to cross the Darién Gap will never be known, but it is next to impossible to speak to anyone who has been through the jungle without receiving a rundown of all the *muertos* they encountered en route. This is to say nothing of the armed assault, rape, and other sexual violence that has become par for the Darién course.

It would not be until January 2024, a full two and a half years after my stint in Siglo XXI, that I would enter the Darién Gap. This I did after spending various months endeavoring to come to terms with the possibility of digital penetration—or worse—in the forest, a common practice deployed by armed assailants against both female and male migrants in the hopes of finding money tucked away in the vagina or anus. Indeed, as if folks who are forced to traverse thousands of kilometers in search of political and economic safety were not already in a sufficiently punishing state of precarious vulnerability, they must also effectively relinquish control over the boundaries of their own bodies. In the end, the unilateral sacrosanctity of the U.S. border not only violates the dignity of the inhabitants of the world who, relegated by the global capitalist order to the lower echelons of humanity, are sentenced to "illegal" migration. It amounts to a physical violation, as well.

Obviously, I lived to tell the tale of the Darién Gap, and my incursion into the jungle did not have to be succeeded by weeks or months of navigating hostile terrain in Central America and Mexico to reach the United States. I did not have to suffer repeated extortion by police and other officials, serve as robbing or kidnapping prey for gangs and cartels, or board La Bestia, Mexico's notorious "train of death," which delivers surviving passengers to the front lines of the bipartisan U.S. war on migrants: the border itself, where the Donald Trumps and the Joe Bidens alike have labored to disappear the very concept of asylum.

And yet the Darién Gap is an extension of this very border in its own right, albeit featuring none of the AI-equipped surveillance towers, drones, and other high-tech accoutrements that define the modern-day U.S.-Mexico frontier. There are no impending "robot dogs" to speak of or other creatures of dystopian fantasy like Texas governor and xenophobe extraordinaire Greg Abbott, the source of such comments as: "The only thing that we're not doing [in Texas] is we're not shooting people who come across the border, because of course, the Biden administration would charge us with murder."[3]

The Darién is instead a place where lawlessness and nature have combined to produce a landscape many migrants refer to as *el infierno verde*, or "the green hell." But at least in terms of dehumanizing deadliness, it is a most twenty-first-century border indeed.

In his 1816 sonnet "On First Looking into Chapman's Homer," Romantic poet John Keats concluded his ode to Chapman's feat of translation by likening the reader's experience to that of "stout Cortez when with eagle eyes / He star'd at the Pacific—and all his men / Look'd at each other with a wild surmise—/ Silent, upon a peak in Darien."

I first read this poem circa 1997 in my high school English class in Austin, Texas, the subject matter of which did not interest me as much as the young instructor, who served as the source of my every waking fantasy. At the time, I had a vague concept of the Darién with its poetically envisioned peak, as my father had spent a portion of his youth in the Panama Canal Zone, where his own father had served the U.S. Department of Defense in various capacities, including as the director of military intelligence for the U.S. Southern Command. The Panamanian Darién hosted the first successful European settlement on the continental Americas, founded by the Spaniards in 1510 and christened Santa María la Antigua del Darién; nowadays, "Darién" can refer to the jungle region spanning Panama and Colombia or to Panama's easternmost province by the same name.

I do not recall whether I knew in 1997 that Keats had been slightly misguided, and that the inaugural eagle-eyed glimpse of the Pacific had not belonged to "stout Cortez"—who in the sixteenth century was busy slaughtering and looting in Mexico—but rather to another horrible Spaniard by the name of Vasco Núñez de Balboa, who crossed the Isthmus of Darién in 1513 with "all his men" in search of gold, trade routes, and other goodies. Centuries later, in keeping with good old colonial continuity, Balboa's surname would be given to the Canal Zone high school my dad attended—the same high school where on January 9, 1964, Panamanian students committed the unpardonable act of attempting to raise the Panamanian flag next to the U.S. one. In the ensuing riots, U.S. forces in the Canal Zone killed at least twenty-one Panamanians.

As part of his civilizing mission in the new world, Balboa presided over the obligatory massacres of Indigenous folks, among them one canine-perpetrated massacre of perceived "sodomites" in 1513 that took place just prior to the sighting of the Pacific. Balboa's dog Leoncico, the offspring of fellow conquistador Juan Ponce de León's dog Becerrillo, reportedly led the attack, summarized as follows by Uruguayan writer Eduardo Galeano in his book *Genesis: Memory of Fire, Volume 1*:

> Tonight, by order of Captain Balboa, the dogs will sink their teeth into the naked flesh of fifty Indians of Panama. They will disembowel and devour fifty who were guilty of the abominable sin of sodomy, *who only lacked tits and wombs to be women.* The spectacle will take place in this mountain clearing, among the trees that the storm uprooted a few days ago. By torchlight the soldiers quarrel and jockey for the best places.
>
> Vasco Núñez de Balboa chairs the ceremony. His dog Leoncico heads up God's avengers. Leoncico, son of Becerrillo, has a body crisscrossed with scars. He is a past master of capturings and quarterings. He gets a sublieutenant's pay and a share of each gold or slave booty.
>
> In two days' time Balboa will discover the Pacific Ocean.[1]

Some contemporary observers have nonetheless detected a silver lining in Balboa's Panamanian operations. In 2013, in honor of the 500th anniversary of the conquistador's transisthmian trek, U.S. journalist Franz Lidz undertook to retrace his footsteps through the Darién on behalf of *Smithsonian Magazine*, noting in the resulting dispatch that "none of the native peoples Balboa encountered in 1513 exist in 2013" and that the Darién is currently populated by groups who migrated there over the past several hundred years. Quoting former Panama City mayor and self-celebrated environmentalist Juan Carlos Navarro on how "diseases and colonial wars brought by the Europeans basically wiped out the Indian populations," Lidz went on to relay Navarro's environmental impact assessment of Spanish colonialism on the mountainous rainforest: "The Indians had stripped much of the jungle to plant corn. In a strange way, the human holocaust Balboa unleashed was the Darién's salvation."[2]

Holocaust notwithstanding, the United States would later select Balboa's name to bestow on the administrative capital of the Canal Zone as well as my dad's high school. One of Panama's most prominent beers is also called Balboa, as is the country's official currency—although the balboa is deemed worthy of existence only in coin form, while all serious transactions requiring actual banknotes are conducted in U.S. dollars. As for the European voyager whose identity is more or less synonymous with Indigenous annihilation, Panama boasts a central province named Colón for Christopher Columbus, the capital city of which is also Colón. For a time in the 1800s, the Americans insisted on calling the city Aspinwall after one of the builders of what is now known as the Panama Canal Railway, behavior that the government of Colombia—to which Panama still belonged—discouraged by blocking the delivery of all mail addressed to Aspinwall.

Along with rainforest preservation activities, Panama's first Spaniards oversaw the widespread use of slavery. In *African Maroons in Sixteenth-Century Panama: A History in Documents*, Robert C. Schwaller writes that by the mid-1520s, Indigenous labor had become so scarce in the nascent colony that "residents began to import Native peoples enslaved during the conquests of

Nicaragua, Guatemala, Mexico, and Peru." When even these imported slaves failed to get the job done in terms of fulfilling labor demands, "Spaniards began to demand enslaved Africans to bolster the available labor supply," and in 1527 "the crown authorized the sale of one thousand Africans to the region" to assist with the construction of Panama City, among other projects.[3] Nor would the perks of forced labor later be lost on the Americans, who would rely heavily on dark-skinned bodies and chaingang servitude in the construction of the Panama Canal, during which countless thousands of lives were lost in the quest to bend the earth to imperial will.

A significant percentage of African slaves escaped Spanish captivity and fled into the forest to form *cimarrón* (maroon) communities, which set about attacking the Spanish forces and effectively wrested control of Darién province from Spain for much of the second half of the sixteenth century. In their Spaniard-antagonizing endeavors, the *cimarrones* intermittently teamed up with English and French pirates, whose incursions further expanded the list of international visitors to the Darién and environs in the half-millennium prior to the region's conversion into an international migration hot spot.

Of course, today's migrants aren't seeking to conquer territory, enslave anyone in gold mines, or commit any other sort of plunder, although certain unhinged members of the American commentariat have determined to expose even more sinister motives among U.S.-bound refuge seekers. In February 2024, white nationalist and self-defined "proud Islamophobe" Laura Loomer—whom Donald Trump once praised as "very special"—descended upon Panama "for a week long trip to the Darién Gap to report on the invasion of America and make the case for why President Trump's America First policies are the solution to the immigration crisis in our country," as she explained on February 11 in her funding appeal on the platform formerly known as Twitter. As of March 1, the GiveSendGo crowdfunding website reported a total of $27,464 raised on behalf of the "Loomer Unleashed in Darién

Gap" campaign, although from our intrepid journalist's bazillion attendant social media posts it appears she did not manage to venture much beyond the migrant reception centers that lie entirely outside the jungle.

In the eyes of her online fan club of devoted sociopaths, however, Loomer's Darién pseudo-expedition was a rousing success. Not only did she observe an alarming "Bank of China" sign while leaving the Panama City airport, but she also got to unleash herself against an array of defenseless migrants who had just emerged from a deadly forest and who unlike Loomer did not have the option to crowdfund their movement across Panama by peddling lucrative conspiracy theories. Plus, she had the full attention and collaboration of Oriel Ortega, the director general of Panama's National Border Service, who confirmed to her that there was indeed an "invasion" going down—although she was hardly the first delirious mega-xenophobe to have the red carpet rolled out by the Panamanian powers that be. Her companion Michael Yon, a U.S. Special Forces veteran and the source of the idea that migrants are orchestrating a "planet of the apes style invasion" with the aim of subjecting the white race to "genocide and cannibalism," has made a name for himself in and around the Darién Gap, where he has also accompanied concerned U.S. congressmen on tours of the incipient apocalypse.[4]

Among Loomer's unsuspecting victims in 2024 was "a bus full of invaders from Africa" whom she accosted in front of the San Vicente migrant camp in the town of Metetí in Darién province, where numerous Panamanian government–arranged buses depart on a daily basis to transport arriving migrants onward to the border with Costa Rica. (That the Pan-American Highway runs directly in front of the San Vicente camp might have alerted Loomer to the fact that she was presently located outside the Darién Gap rather than in the middle of a roadless jungle.) Appallingly, "several of the Africans were wearing tribal outfits." There were also plenty of encounters with "Venezuelan invaders," one of whom was sporting an Obama hat. As if any more incriminating evidence was needed, other invading Venezuelans reportedly told Loomer that Trump was "a bitch" and that they loved Biden. Then there were some men from Afghanistan who "openly admitted" that they were journeying to the United States and Canada "to 'escape the Taliban,'" the obvious moral of the story being that it was "only a matter of time before we have another 9/11 style terrorist attack in our country." Finally, there was the "Chinese invader" in San Vicente who via a mobile phone translation app claimed to be from Beijing and "said he was traveling with 2 children"—living proof that "the Chinese Communist party is actively invading the U.S. via invaders. And they are coming in via the Darien Gap."[5]

While U.S. Democrats deploy slightly more refined rhetoric than "invading invader" babble, they are pretty militantly anti-"invasion," too—and not just in terms of Biden's efforts to out-Trump Trump in construction of the "Big, Beautiful" border wall. In October 2023, New York City mayor Eric Adams exercised his entitlement to swift and easy cross-border movement in order to swing through the Colombian coastal city of Necoclí, which lies just east of the Darién Gap across the Gulf of Urabá and is a primary jumping-off point for migrants heading into the jungle. In comments made before a crowd of hundreds of migrants by the Necoclí boat dock, *The New York Times* reported, Adams "alluded to difficult conditions 'on the streets of New York'" and thereby sought to deter folks from continuing their planned trajectory.[6] Obviously, Adams's deterrence strategy worked just as well as that time Biden's vice president, Kamala Harris, flew down to Central America to lecture anyone considering fleeing poverty and violence: "Do not come."[7] After all, it's difficult to deter people who have nothing to lose, although it's a lot easier to ensure that their journeys remain unnecessarily complicated and dangerous.

From Necoclí, boats depart for the Colombian villages of Acandí and Capurganá, where migrants then set out on foot into the forest, emerging on the Panamanian side anywhere from a few days to a few weeks later—if they emerge at all, that is. There are other less trafficked and more costly routes, as well, such as by boat from Capurganá to the Panamanian villages of Carreto and Caledonia, which lie northwest of Acandí and Capurganá. These routes entail far less walking and, by all accounts, fewer perils; as four young men from Afghanistan who had gone via Carreto told me when I spoke to them in Tapachula in November 2023, they had encountered no dead people and no animals along the way, and they hadn't even been robbed yet—although they still had all of Mexico ahead of them. The men showed me a cell phone video of their boat ride from Necoclí, in which they flashed the obligatory grins and thumbs-up signs as the vessel crashed recklessly through the waves, and for the duration of our conversation exhibited a disproportionate grace that I myself surely would not have been able to muster had I gone from being a victim of the U.S. war on terror on one side of the world to a victim of the U.S. war on migrants on the other.

Caledonia is another potentially less lethal option for navigating the Darién, unless your boat sinks, and is named for a disastrous Scottish colonial experiment at the tail end of the seventeenth century. In 1698, William Paterson, himself the founder of the Bank of England, convinced a bunch of other Scots that they should go try their hand at erecting "New Edinburgh" on the coast of Panama west of the Gulf of Darién, in what they named the Bay of Caledonia—the starting point, as it so happens, for Balboa's 1513 transisthmian expedition. Paterson's "Proposal to Plant a Colony in Darien" advertised the region as holding the veritable "keys of the universe" for global commerce: "These doors of the seas and the keys of the universe would of course be capable of enabling their possessors to give laws to both oceans, and to become the arbitrators of the commercial world, without being liable to the fatigues, expenses, and dangers, or of contracting such guilt and blood, as Alexander and Caesar."[8]

The initial batch of twelve hundred Scots sailed to Darién loaded up with all sorts of provisions guaranteed to jump-start their quest for global trading power status. According to Martin

Mitchinson's book *The Darien Gap: Travels in the Rainforest of Panama*, these included 300 tons of biscuits, 15 tons of pork, 5,000 gallons of brandy, 1,700 gallons of rum, 1,700 gallons of strong claret, 1,440 Scotch bonnets "delivered as a first instalment on the contract for an even larger order," 1,500 English Bibles, and "tartan hose, stocking, and boxes with four thousand periwigs, bobwigs, and campaign wigs."[9]

Less than two years later, "Nueva Caledonia" was no longer, having been defeated by disease, starvation, torrential rains and heat, attacks by the Spaniards—who had gotten their panties into a royal bunch over the colonial competition—and an English ban on trade with the aspiring "arbitrators of the commercial world." Many of the colonists had perished, among them Paterson's wife. One of the survivors, the Reverend Francis Borland, issued an indignant moral condemnation of the Panamanian territory: "Darien is pernicious, unwholesome and contagious. Thou devourest men and eatest up thy inhabitants."[10]

The colony's impressive failure spelled economic cataclysm for Scotland, requiring a bailout from none other than the Bank of England and leading to the kingdom's renunciation of political independence in 1707. And yet there was plenty more historical irony to come. Another survivor of the so-called Darién Scheme, a certain Rev. Alexander Stobo, would eventually make his genealogical mark as the great-great-great-great-grandfather of Theodore Roosevelt, honorary midwife of the nation of Panama, which was severed from Colombia—with crucial assistance from the gringos—during Roosevelt's presidency in 1903. National sovereignty got off to an excellent start when the task of raising the new Panamanian flag was allocated to an officer in the U.S. Army Corps of Engineers.

Immediately following Panamanian "independence," the United States acquired its latest de facto colony in the form of the Panama Canal Zone, over which it would enjoy unfettered rule until the Canal Zone's official termination in 1979—although it would not be until 1999 that control of the canal was formally handed over to Panama. The canal itself was completed in 1914, the Americans having triumphed, at an enormous cost in money and human life, where the French had failed, also at an enormous cost in money and human life. In his exhaustive tome *The Path Between the Seas: The Creation of the Panama Canal 1870–1914*, historian David McCullough details Roosevelt's obsession with the canal as "the vital—the *indispensable*—path to a global destiny for the United States of America." The Rooseveltian vision, McCullough writes, was "of his country as the commanding power on two oceans, and these joined by a canal built, owned, operated, policed and fortified by his country."[11] In other words, perhaps, it was Paterson's "doors of the seas and the keys of the universe" all over again.

As coincidence would have it, McCullough begins his six-hundred-plus-page story in the Darién, which for a spell starting in the mid-1800s had been regarded as perhaps an ideal spot for the coveted interoceanic canal; Nicaragua and the Mexican Isthmus of Tehuantepec were also considered, before the waterway's actual location was settled on west of the Darién on the Isthmus of Panama. The extensive interest displayed in the Darién option by the governments of Britain, France, and the United States was thanks in good part to the overly active imagination of one Dr. Edward Cullen, an Irish physician who, having failed to strike it rich in the California gold rush, devised in 1850 another potential international side hustle in reviving the defunct Spanish gold mines in Panama.

This was not to pan out, either, but in the course of trying to woo the London-based Royal Geographical Society with his mining visions, Cullen managed to instead spark a Darién canal rush, if you will, by pathologically inflating his own familiarity with the Panamanian landscape. Among his topographical hallucinations was that traversal of the Darién was a piece of cake and that the isthmus was in fact "so narrow" that one could simultaneously view the Atlantic and Pacific Oceans. Additionally, there were no serious elevation issues impeding canal construction. These fanciful notions and more made it into two editions of Cullen's work *The Isthmus of Darién Ship Canal*.

As Todd Balf notes in his book *The Darkest Jungle: The True Story of the Darién Expedition and America's Ill-Fated Race to Connect the Seas*, the Darién Gap itself was also previously called Cullen's Gap after the eponymous "rogue figure" and was "defined altogether differently" in the mid-nineteenth century than it would be later on—as the sought-after "low spot in the coast-running mountains." When in the 1960s the Darién Gap began drawing "hordes of bandana-clad backpackers who . . . saw something sacrosanct in the blot of roadless rain forest" dividing the continents, the "Gap" would be newly understood as the break in the "paved dagger of civilization" known as the Pan-American Highway.[12]

The ill-fated U.S. Darién Exploring Expedition charted by Balf took place in 1854, when, encouraged by Cullen's ostensible findings as well as some similarly misguided assessments courtesy of the English engineer Lionel Gisborne, the U.S. Navy dispatched a contingent of men to check out canal prospects in the Darién. Led by a young lieutenant named Isaac Strain, the expeditionary party set out from Caledonia Bay, site of the Scottish demise, for what was meant to be an expedited survey but turned into a two-month exercise in physical and psychological torment. The group became hopelessly lost in the jungle, forced to contend with such indomitable forces of nature as the Chucunaque River, which, as Balf writes, was "all chaos, the product of the freakishly large volume of rain" that falls annually on the Darién.[13]

Progressively the men lost their clothing, minds, and tooth enamel, the final substance a casualty of a diet overly reliant on palm nuts. They also became acquainted with botflies, larval mosquito-borne parasites that embed under the skin and go about gorging themselves on bodily tissue. Notes Balf: "River bathing produced the most excruciating episodes because the maggot, which employs a snorkel-like apparatus to breathe, feels its air supply shut off and begins to writhe, using its sharp anal hooks to mobilize."[14] Not all of the expeditioners survived; Strain ended up losing half his body weight. The Yale-educated Theodore Winthrop, another survivor who would go on to die in the U.S. Civil War, wrote at one point during the journey: "Life is of very little value to me, as I shall never accomplish anything in it, but there is something very desperate in the tho't of a death in this wilderness."[15]

The ultimate upshot of the Darién Exploring Expedition was that there was no "gap" for a canal, after all, although it would still be another sixteen or so years before the issue was definitively put to rest—and not without various last stands by Cullen, including a disgruntled 1856 book concisely titled *Over Darién by a Ship Canal: Reports of the Mismanaged Darién Expedition of 1854, with Suggestions for a Survey by Competent Engineers, and an Exploration by Parties with Compasses*. More than a century later, in the 1960s, the idea of an interoceanic passageway in the Darién would surface once again, as the United States explored the possibility of nuclear bombing a bigger and better sea-level canal into existence in eastern Panama. In September 1964 (less than twenty years after Hiroshima and Nagasaki), a *New York Times* headline gushed in anticipation of "A New Canal—Dug by Atom Bombs."

According to the *Times*, "about 325 nuclear explosives of varying yields would be used" in the undertaking, which had become all the more attractive a proposal in the aftermath of the "anti-American rioting in the Canal Zone" over the Balboa High School flag-raising incident earlier that year. There was no danger, apparently, of engendering anti-American sentiment by simply nuking a large swath of Panamanian territory that was home to thousands of Indigenous persons, and the *Times* assured readers that U.S. Atomic Energy Commission experts were "convinced . . . that radioactivity need not be a hazard." The nuclear plan was eventually shelved, but as per the Manual website the U.S. military did manage to litter the Darién Gap with loads of unexploded ordnance during the Cold War, the fallout of aerial training runs over the jungle.

The Oregon-based website—which purports to be "The Essential Guide for Men" and offers advice on tying ties, shaping beards, and finding the best masculine sweaters—lists undetonated munitions as but one of the many "things that will kill you" inside the Darién Gap. Also on the list are fer-de-lance pit vipers, Brazilian wandering spiders, jungle heat, dirty water, trench foot, and croco-diles. The Manual credits British army officer Gavin Thompson as having led the very first successful vehicle expedition across the deadly Gap—as part of the 1971–72 British Trans-Americas Expedition—with two Range Rovers and a bevy of engineers and scientists to help coax the automobiles through the antagonistic terrain. The vehicular crossing took nearly one hundred days, and yet it was hardly the first of its kind; *Land Rover Monthly*, for one, has found it necessary to highlight the "fundamental falsehood of this remarkable claim."[16]

In 1960, a dozen years before Thompson and company braved the Gap, the Trans-Darién Expedition had already been conducted with an eye to scouting a route for the missing link in the Pan-American Highway. *Land Rover Monthly* reports that, with a Land Rover station wagon nicknamed *La Cucaracha Cariñosa* ("The Cute Cockroach") and a Jeep pickup in tow, the Trans-Darién team reached an average speed of 201 meters per hour. The magazine adds that "other sources" attribute the Darién Gap's first success-ful vehicular navigation to three Brazilians—two military officers and a mechanic—who set out from Rio de Janeiro in 1928, turn-ing up ten years later in Detroit.

The Darién Gap has also played host to all manner of other adventures beyond the established conquest, plunder, and canal pursuits of centuries past. In 2001, for example, British ex-paratrooper Karl Bushby crossed the Gap as part of his ongoing mission to walk around the world "with unbroken footsteps," a project he has termed the "Goliath Expedition." The Darién was the first of three worldly "gaps that created uncertainty" for Bushby—the others being the Bering Strait and the English Channel—and landed him in a Panamanian jail for eighteen days on account of unauthorized movement in a border zone frequented by Colombian guerrillas. A different sort of Darién mission was embarked upon by Richard Oglesby Marsh, an adventurous Amer-ican engineer, ethnologist, and dabbler in diplomatic affairs who in 1924 and 1925 went tromping through the jungle in search of a race of white Indians. Marsh, whose published works comprised "Blond Indians of the Darien Jungle" and *White Indians of Darien*, claimed to have seen no fewer than four hundred of these white-skinned "savages" during his second expedition, after which he brought "back to civilization two boys and a girl as living specimens for the scientists to study." A charming photo outside the New Willard Hotel in Washington, D.C., depicts Marsh, his wife, and the "specimens" decked out in excruciatingly civilized attire.

In short, there has been no shortage over the ages of human beings who have crossed the Darién Gap entirely by choice rather than out of necessity. But for the many inhabitants of the world who are denied the privilege of being able to choose to pursue adventure for adventure's sake, the Cuban assessment that I scribbled in my notebook in the Siglo XXI jail still applies: "Cubans say no one leaves their country and walks thru selva for a week if they don't have to." Meanwhile, the roster of folks who can afford to walk through the selva because they want to is also populated by the likes of aforementioned authors Martin Mitchinson and Todd Balf, who staged respective modern-day expeditions into the Darién—Mitchinson's of a far more protracted and objectively successful nature than Balf's. I, too, would later conduct my own short-lived incursion into the jungle, which while obviously also done from a position of extreme privilege was less of an adventure than an exercise in terrifying the fuck out of myself.

To be sure, some of the Darién's voluntary visitors have been memorialized as more wacky than necessarily heroic, but there persists a general respect for the adventurer's physical feat of confronting the jungle, be it in the manner of Vasco Núñez de Balboa, Isaac Strain, or Karl Bushby. This same respect is conspicuously absent from contemporary appraisals of migrant trajectories in the Darién Gap, regardless of the downright awe-inspiring feats these crossings often entail. As Tamara Guillermo, a field coordinator for Doctors Without Borders, commented to me during one of my visits to Panama, the trans-Darién trek would be difficult enough "for an Olympic athlete," much less improperly equipped humans in less than prime physical condition. The more than half a million people who survived the Darién in 2023 included elderly persons and babies; nearly one in four migrants were children. I personally have met Darién survivors with physical afflictions that render the mere act of walking challenging but who somehow navigated mountains, rivers, and all-consuming mud to make it through. The same cannot be said of the "Colombian force of some two thousand men" who, McCullough notes, "did attempt an overland march through the Darien wilderness" on the occasion of the creation of Panama in 1903, "but ravaged by fever, they gave up and turned back."[17] Per McCullough's calculations, the Republic of Panama nonetheless "probably would not have lasted a week" without the convenient presence of American gunboats off the Panamanian coast.[18]

And while more and more people are now finding it imperative to leave their homes and walk through the selva in the direction of hoped-for eventual safety, it bears underscoring that trans-Darién migration is hardly a new phenomenon. Indigenous residents of the Panamanian and Colombian Darién, for instance, traditionally had little use for the borders of nation-states and the obstacles to human movement that they ostensibly signify. The Kuna people and the Emberá and Wounaan tribes, the latter two known collectively as the Chocó, migrated to Panama at different times in history from what is now Colombia. The same tribes continue to exist on the Colombian side of the border, as well, where the department containing the Colombian Darién is also called Chocó.[19]

Moreover, the jungle route has been utilized for decades by refugees fleeing political and economic oppression, including Colombians displaced by the never-ending civil war that began in 1964 and that has provided a certain global superpower with plenty of opportunities to fuel bloodshed. During the presidential reign of far-right narco-politician Álvaro Uribe (2002–10), the United States flung gargantuan sums of money at the country while its military went about slaughtering thousands of peasants and passing the corpses off as left-wing guerrillas. In return for artificially inflating the body count of dead guerrillas in order to justify yet more U.S. military aid to Colombia, soldiers received monetary rewards, extra holiday time, and other perks. Uribe followed up his blood-drenched presidency with a professorship at Georgetown University in Washington, D.C.

While conducting research in the Darién in the mid-1980s, American ethnographer Stephanie Kane noted the regularity with which the jungle was already being transited by people just seeking to make a living. Consider a passage from Kane's book *The Phantom Gringo Boat: Shamanic Discourse and Development in Panama*, in which she recounts a 1984 encounter on the Panamanian side of the jungle:

> We meet a young black man who had just accomplished the arduous journey across the mountains from the [Colombian] Chocó in three days. An Evangelical agriculturist looking for work, he tells how years of travel through Venezuela and Ecuador have kept him in good physical shape. Like other migrants who pass briefly through this first human settlement on the Panamanian side, he is given a day's food in exchange for a day's work and heads off downriver to highway and city.[20]

On another occasion, Kane and her companion happen upon "another couple of poor souls"—one of them Colombian, one Peruvian—who arrive in Panama "half-dead" from the cross-border trek: "They'd been walking six days, the last two with no food. They even tried to eat plantains green. We were the first people they'd seen since their guide, taking a watch in payment, took them over the pass and told them Panama was two days down, that way." When Kane speaks with the duo again the following day, she reports that their "bodies seem to be recovering, but their minds were definitely blown. They'd seen skeletons propped up against trees and clothes strewn all along (wet clothes rub skin raw). Since they didn't know the way, they'd come straight down the river, steep, forceful, rocky. They were scared out of their minds, especially at night, when they slept on little dry islands in the river: they might easily have been swept away."[21]

Forty years later, the same story continues to play out in the Darién on a daily basis, only on a far more massive scale. Guides take their payment and abandon migrants, skin is rubbed raw, food runs out, the river sweeps people away. Minds are blown and fear reigns, as skeletons and much fresher corpses serve as constant reminders of the very short distance between life and death for those denied the luxury of crossing borders at will. As one Venezuelan refuge seeker commented matter-of-factly to me when I spoke with her and her extended family of ten in Tapachula: "I can say that we have all stepped on dead people."

Like almost all of the U.S.-bound migrants I have ever conversed with, this woman was not in pursuit of an "American dream" replete with fancy cars, houses, and other riches; rather, the dream was simply to reach a geographic location where economic survival was at least within the realm of possibility. In her family's case, the ultimate goal was to return to Venezuela, a geography decimated by U.S. sanctions, with enough money to make survival there possible, too.

Alas, even the modified American dream requires migrants to pass through an extended nightmare, which, if navigated successfully, deposits them in the American nightmare itself: a country where, opportunities for relatively profitable undocumented labor aside, there is nothing much to write home about in terms of basic rights or humanity. Trillions of dollars are funneled into the arms industry and waging wars against manufactured nemeses abroad, while fundamental human needs—such as less than criminally expensive health care, education, and housing options— are nowhere to be found on the list of domestic priorities.

Meanwhile, of the countless refuge seekers who set out for the U.S. border but never arrive, an untold number end up skeletons on a roadless stretch of territory at the crossroads of the Americas, left to ride out eternity silent, upon a peak in Darién.

The day before he entered the Darién Gap with three companions and a vision of reaching the apartment of an acquaintance in Boston, Massachusetts, Johan had a dream about the jungle. He was crossing a river and was assaulted by a group of men, whom he and his friend Andrés had to fight. "The Darién was always on my mind; I was always thinking about it," he would later tell me by way of explaining the source of his dream, which *gracias a Dios* did not play out in reality. "*Gracias a Dios* nothing happened to us, except that we didn't have anything to eat."

I met Johan, a twenty-one-year-old from Caracas, on February 26, 2023, in the Indigenous village of Bajo Chiquito on the Panamanian side of the Darién Gap, shortly after he emerged from the jungle. It was not until seven months later in September, however, that he would recount to me the Darién crossing in full detail. In the intervening months, he traversed Central America and Mexico, the final four days of which journey were spent incommunicado atop La Bestia, while I sobbed on the floor of my apartment in Zipolite and imagined every possible horror. Having become constant WhatsApp correspondents with Johan and the rest of his group, which in Panama had grown from four to nine Colombians and Venezuelans but then shrunk to seven in Costa Rica, I had made it my mission to get them to the border of my homeland if for no other reason than to spite the system. My efforts mainly entailed having a continuous neurotic breakdown while begging people to send me money so that I might engage in interminable battles with Western Union to send it on to the Colombo-Venezuelans, who used the funds for bus fare, food, and myriad extortion payments.

On April 8, Johan and his friends crossed from the northern Mexican border city of Ciudad Juárez, where I had met them for one night involving a preposterous amount of beer and precarious salsa dancing, into El Paso, Texas, and were instantly apprehended by the U.S. *migra*. The Colombians in the group were released into the land of the free after a brief detention, while the Venezuelans were held in Texas for six days—during which time they were permitted a single shower—and then flown, cuffed at the hands and feet, to Arizona, where they were dumped back over the border into Nogales in the Mexican state of Sonora.

Following some disconcerting run-ins between Johan and organized crime in Nogales, I managed to persuade him that the United States sucked anyway and that he could travel to Spain, instead, which wasn't necessarily great either but which passport-holding Venezuelans could at least reach visa-free and without risk to life and limb. The issue of Johan's lack of said travel document could not, it turned out, be resolved in timely fashion at the Venezuelan embassy in Mexico City due to a shortage of passport production materials, as a friendly sexagenarian embassy official explained to me. But not to fear: Johan could fly to Caracas, for a minimal fee, on a special repatriation flight operated by the Venezuelan airline Conviasa, whereupon he could sort his passport in a jiffy and be off to Spain. My new embassy friend was thrilled to learn that my wardrobe included a pink Hugo Chávez T-shirt acquired during one of my visits to the country in 2009, and he helped to expedite Johan's repatriation process in between sending me selfies, Chávez tributes, and virtual kisses to my neck and back.

Johan arrived home at his Caracas barrio on May 3, a place he had not seen in more than four years on account of employment on a coca plantation in the Catatumbo region of the Colombian department of Norte de Santander, where in lucky months he had earned a few hundred dollars—which was still more than he could hope to earn at home. He would often pick 60 to 80 kilos of coca leaves per day, a harvest that had to be hauled up and down mountains and that had left him with white scars on his hands and back, which he attributed to the chemicals utilized on the crops. His colleague and Darién companion Andrés had been left with a hernia. Johan's coca-picking days were immortalized in a fast-motion video, set to Latin trap music, of him in a red hoodie against a bright green hillside, yanking up leaves and stuffing them into a basket fastened to his waist. Coca cultivation in this sector of Catatumbo took place under the auspices of remnants of the Revolutionary Armed Forces of Colombia (FARC), the guerrilla organization that formed in the 1960s in response to institutionalized socioeconomic injustice in the country. According to Johan, it was generally preferable to toil on behalf of the FARC than right-wing paramilitaries, even if the guerrillas had made him cut off his braids. Paramilitary operations in Catatumbo had included perpetrating more than 115 massacres and 5,000 killings between 1999 and 2004 alone, as per a report by Colombia's National Center for Historical Memory.

In Caracas Johan was reunited with his mother and almost five-year-old daughter, who lived with her own mother and maternal grandmother but was allowed to spend a good deal of time wreaking havoc with her cousins at Johan's mom's place. The swift passport procurement promised to me by my Mexico City embassy buddy was not to be, and Johan instead entered into an existential struggle with the Venezuelan passport gods, who only after four months consented to rescue his file from the bureaucratic black hole into which it had been disappeared.

And so it was that on September 2, Johan joined me in Madrid for a month of cohabitation in an apartment I had rented not far from the Prado, where we consumed a lot of homemade arepas, watched a never-ending Pablo Escobar series on YouTube, played cards, and staged various telenovela-caliber quarrels for the viewing pleasure of the Madrilenian patrons of a crappy bar down the street. Twenty years my junior, Johan's hair was partially dyed platinum; the names of his mother, Nelvis, and daughter, Loriannys, were tattooed on the backs of his upper arms, although Loriannys was missing her S, an oversight by the tattoo artist that Johan had been too embarrassed to correct. When I first met him and his friends in Bajo Chiquito, Johan had assigned the name Loriannys to his WhatsApp account along with the photo of a Puerto Rican rapper, meaning that for the first two weeks of our correspondence I had no idea whom I was corresponding with. What would later turn into a semi-amorous relationship with Johan intermittently caused me to feel like a scary old lady, but it was not usually anything that a few glasses of wine could not resolve.

Madrid was also where, at long last, Johan gave me the blow-by-blow of the February 2023 Darién crossing, which neither of us knew at the time would be merely his first of three incursions into the Gap in the space of a little over a year. His initial attempt at narration of the tale was cut short by an altercation between the two of us over whether it was really possible to cross the jungle from Acandí, Colombia, to Bajo Chiquito in one and a half days, as Johan claimed to have done. The story checked out with his friends, I repented, and he continued his chronicle one sunny afternoon on a bench outside the Prado.

Narration was heavily aided by the word *vaina*, pillar of Venezuelan and Colombian Spanish, which—as an article in the Colombian newspaper *El Tiempo* notes—is a "verbal crutch" as well as a "word that means everything and nothing. . . . 'Vaina' can signify anything but also its opposite, good or bad, tasty or tasteless, pleasant or boring, the sun or the moon, night and day, winter or summer."[22]

In the case of Johan's dream, for example, he wasn't just crossing a river, he was "crossing a river *y vaina*"—the verbal crutch equivalent in English of "crossing a river and whatever." While my journalistic modus operandi for interviews was generally to scribble notes by hand and then not be able to read them, I had Johan record his story into WhatsApp messages to myself on my phone:

ME: OK one two three go.
JOHAN (*in English*): One two three four five six seven.
ME: OK why did you decide to leave Colombia and go to the U.S.?
JOHAN: To look for a better life and help my family. Andrés and I had been planning it for a while but we didn't have the money to leave—well in reality when we left we didn't have money either. But we got El Mono and Felipe and they managed to get four million pesos, which was like six hundred dollars at the time. So we talked to them and planned it and we left on a Monday. The four of us left with four million pesos, which anyway wasn't enough for anything, but we wanted to get out of where we were because it was shit.

El Mono's given name was Wilmer; I persisted for months in thinking that his nickname was "Monkey," before Johan informed me that in Colombia *mono* was also used to designate a fair-skinned person, like *güero* in Mexico. El Mono and Felipe were Catatumbo natives and also employed in the coca industry, El Mono having been high enough up in the hierarchy to have owned a decent motorcycle before losing it to debt. Felipe was the most animated of the group and the one with whom I would coordinate the sending of funds for bus tickets and official extortion payments throughout the length of Central America and Mexico; he was also the group's self-appointed videographer, filming the Darién, La Bestia, and everything in between, to the extent that his cell phone charge permitted. Andrés was Venezuelan like Johan and had been on the verge of becoming a father when his girlfriend gave birth to stillborn female twins while working in the field. Whenever he was overcome with self-doubt about his decision to risk everything to reach the United States, Andrés later told me, his girlfriend would remind him to think of his daughters and never give up.

Felipe and Andrés would eventually end up in Boston in accordance with the original vision, while El Mono landed in Kentucky—or "Qitoqui," as he preferred to spell it.

JOHAN: So we left Catatumbo in Norte de Santander. We bought bus tickets for Medellín, we stayed in a hotel there one night *y vaina*, and then we bought bus tickets for Necoclí, which is where you get the boat to the selva. Necoclí is eight or nine hours from Medellín and when we got there it was all mafia; it was crazy.

ME: Like a cartel or what?

JOHAN: A mafia. The *paracos*, the paramilitaries. We investigated what the *vaina* was with the selva and we went to ask about the boat because when we got to Necoclí they told us it was two hundred and fifty or three hundred dollars per person including a guide, but anyway the guides just charge you and then leave you to get killed or kidnapped or raped because whatever happens in there they are obviously not going to risk their lives for you. What they do is they fuck with your head and since you've never been in the selva before you start thinking, "Oh yeah you're right I need a guide," and they scare you. But obviously you have to see it for yourself to know what it's like. But obviously it's crazy.

ME: But do the guides tell you they'll take you all the way to Panama?

JOHAN: No, just to the flag [denoting the Colombian-Panamanian border].

ME: Because I've talked to people who say the guides tell you they'll take you the whole way and then leave you.

JOHAN: They take you as far as the flag and then they go back the same day. It's all up and down and *vainas* like that but they're used to it. So anyway we got to where they sold the boat tickets from Necoclí to Acandí, and of course it was much cheaper to just buy the boat ticket instead of paying the two hundred and fifty or three hundred dollars they were trying to charge us. So we paid like not even twenty dollars for the boat, although now it's more expensive because you know how these things are. We bought the four tickets and we paid the guy a little bit extra to put us on the boat right away so we wouldn't have to wait. We took off on the boat and it was like two hours to Acandí.

ME: You weren't scared?

JOHAN: Of course I was scared; I don't like water. But I was, you know, praying to God the whole time. We got to Acandí and some people stayed there and others continued on to Capurganá [the other main entrance to the jungle]. We got there broke, with no money at all.

ME: Why did you go to Acandí and not Capurganá?

JOHAN: Because it was cheaper.

ME: But is the Capurganá route safer?

JOHAN: No, it's the same. Because when you go in there in the selva no one is safe. So we got to Acandí; we didn't have money. We stayed there for a day and a half with no food or anything trying to figure out what to do. El Mono and Felipe wanted to go back, but I kept saying I'm not going back and Andrés did too. I told the others go back if you want but we're already here, we're already practically in the selva, why should we go back and be indebted to people? And then a *pana* [another term obsessively deployed in Venezuelan Spanish, meaning "friend"] in the U.S. sent us two hundred dollars and we went and negotiated with the señora, the one in charge of the selva. She was short and fat and she made all the decisions, so we talked to her to see if she would let us pass for two hundred dollars. She said no, that she was going to send us back to Necoclí until we had all of the money, that things were different now and it wasn't like before when you could cross the selva however you wanted, that now it was all organized and controlled by . . . well obviously she didn't say by who. It was like a mini-pueblo where we were in Acandí. The next afternoon we went back to talk to her again, and she said how many people are you and how much money do you have, and then she said OK go get your bags and get out of here,

I don't want to see your faces anymore, and she let us go for two hundred. And they took us in a *motocarro* [auto rickshaw] to a camp where there were people from Haiti, China, Syria, all sorts of countries. Colombians, Venezuelans, from everywhere. We got there at night and slept in the camp, and at six the next morning we entered the selva because we still weren't actually in the selva for real.

ME: How far was the camp from Acandí?

JOHAN: Like twenty minutes.

ME: And you couldn't walk there from Acandí?

JOHAN: Nooooo, because like the señora said if you guys try to do this your own way you'll see what happens to you later on— because in the selva they can fuck you for whatever *vaina*. And you could tell that there were a lot of people around who were *paracos*, who were paramilitaries.

Johan had told me before of the señora—who perhaps on account of the Pablo Escobar YouTube overdose had come to occupy an almost mythical status in my mind, where she starred in her very own narco-series: *La señora de la selva*. The "paramilitaries" Johan was referencing here were most likely affiliated with the Clan del Golfo (the Gulf Clan), a neo-paramilitary outfit and Colombia's dominant drug-trafficking organization, which had detected big bucks in the movement of migrants through the Darién and had taken control of that business as well.

The Clan del Golfo has also been known, among other names, as the Autodefensas Gaitanistas de Colombia (Gaitanista Self-Defense Forces of Colombia, or AGC) and as the Urabeños, in honor of the Urabá region where Necoclí is situated. The term *Gaitanista* derives from the name of Jorge Eliécer Gaitán, the charismatic Liberal Party leader who self-identified as a socialist and whose 1948 assassination in Bogotá earned him his own mythical status in Colombian popular memory. Given Gaitán's opposition to right-wing paramilitary violence, it's not quite clear why the AGC determined that his name would be a good fit for their group, but the appropriation has been publicly challenged by the man's descendants.

Among Gaitán's claims to fame was his activism on behalf of the victims of the 1928 "banana massacre" of striking employees of the United Fruit Company—the U.S. corporation and blood-sucking parasite of Latin America—in the town of Ciénaga on Colombia's northern coast, an episode memorialized in Gabriel García Márquez's *One Hundred Years of Solitude*. Eighty years after the massacre, in 2007, United Fruit's reincarnation Chiquita Brands International was fined $25 million in a Washington, D.C., court for making protection payments to the Autodefensas Unidas de Colombia (United Self-Defense Forces of Colombia, or AUC), the AGC's paramilitary predecessors and a U.S. government–designated Foreign Terrorist Organization. In June 2024, a U.S. federal court ordered Chiquita to pay $38.3 million in compensation to families of victims of the AUC.

JOHAN: We stayed there in the camp outside Acandí, and the next day we started walking at six o'clock in the morning. We walked and we walked and we walked. There were guides; there were several of them. There was one at the front and then after like one hundred people there was another one. But anyway they weren't even necessary because the path is marked with plastic bags and you know which way to go—you have to follow the blue bags, not the red ones. We were always ahead of the group, and we walked walked walked walked walked walked walked—we walked so much and we didn't really rest because like I said we didn't have food so why would we stop to rest. We ate whatever we could find in there, stuff people had thrown on the ground *y vaina*. Or sometimes someone would give you something.

Then we got to a mountain that took two hours to climb; it took forever. But since we didn't have kids with us or anything, we were faster than other people. We passed people who had been walking for five days, six days, seven days, eight days—they

would ask us, How long have you been walking? We would
say we left this morning and they would say oh we've been in
here for five or six days. People with kids, old people, people
with crutches.

ME: Did you see animals?

JOHAN: We didn't see any but of course they're there. Snakes,
jaguars, everything, all kinds of animals because obviously it's a
selva. We kept walking and we went up that mountain without
stopping to rest at all. We went up and up and up until we got to
the top, *gracias a Dios*. But then we had to go up another one
and another one. Later we had to cross a bunch of rivers but
they weren't too high because it wasn't raining, *gracias a Dios*.

Having myself been disabused of religion by the Catholic
schoolteachers in Texas who had taught me that my dog was not
going to heaven, it had taken me a while to get used to the non-
stop invocation of God by Johan, his friends, and his mother, with
whom I spent the six days of his detention in El Paso Whats-
Apping about how, God willing, he would be released the next
day and how God had put me in her path to take care of her son
(no pressure). Nor did I find it enormously reassuring when God
was put in charge of dealing with my numerous concerns, such as
that Johan and his buddies would fall asleep atop La Bestia and
end up decapitated on the tracks (ME: Please do not fall asleep on
La Bestia and end up decapitated. JOHAN AND BUDDIES:
With the grace of God we will not). Eventually, however, I fell
into the habit of thanking God for everything, too, like when
Johan was finally presented with his Venezuelan passport and
when all the necessary arepa-making materials were located in
the neighborhood supermarket in Madrid.

JOHAN: We continued walking. We ended up having to rest like
three times because we had walked so much. Inside the selva
they were setting up little stores to sell water, soft drinks, bread,
and *vainas* like that, but it's all a mafia and they charge whatever

they want because people have no choice. We continued walking and walking and that same day we passed the flag [on the Colombian-Panamanian border]. Well there's two flags and a cross at the top of a mountain, and when we got there we rested a bit and checked out the *vaina*. From there down is Panama.

We rested and then we continued on because we wanted to get out of there as fast as possible, obviously, because like I said we had no food or water—we had to drink river water contaminated with all the *muertos*.

ME: And you saw *muertos*?

JOHAN: Obviously we saw *muertos*. There was a woman who gave birth to twins in the selva, and she died in a tent with the two babies. She bled to death and there was no one to help her, no doctor or anyone else. But who would stop to help anyone anyway? If you stop to help you'll never get out, there are so many people who need help—people with children, old people. There were even men who went with their wives and abandoned them in the middle of the selva and kept going. I know this because I saw it with my own eyes.

ME: And how many *muertos* did you see?

JOHAN: Several. . . . There was the girl with the twins, there was a dead man whose face was already being eaten by worms, there was a fat man floating dead in the river. He was an older man, like forty years old.

ME: Really old, like me.

JOHAN: Yeah. Well I don't know how old he was but I'd guess forty or so. But he was fat and he was floating down the river, dead. That's why you shouldn't drink that water.

Johan was not the only Darién survivor I spoke to who posited the existence of a certain law of the jungle, as it were, according to which it was every man for himself and you couldn't afford to stop and help anyone. A young Colombian man named Josmar, who had crossed the Darién Gap via Acandí in 2022 and whose acquaintance I made in Mexico, similarly stressed to me that "it's either your life or another person's life," contending that any energy expended on another human being could mean your own demise. This had not prevented Josmar from rescuing a baby swept from his mother's arms by the river current; nor had it stopped him from sharing his last bit of bread with a desperately hungry child. In Johan's case, too, his solidary tendencies in the jungle contradicted his own bleak analysis.

JOHAN: From the flag we kept going; we had to go down this horrible descent.

It was horrible, horrible. There was a rope you had to hold onto while going down and it was really tough; not everyone can go down something like that, you know? That's where I helped this girl who had a kid with her who was like two or three. The girl was a little overweight and she was really suffering, so I offered to help her for nothing in return but she told me no, that she wanted to give me something for helping her. Felipe and El Mono went ahead but Andrés stayed more or less with me, and I helped the girl and the kid down that horrible *vaina*, and everyone kept saying how we have to get to the river, we have to get to the river. I carried the kid on my shoulder and finally we got to the river. The girl gave me twenty dollars and Andrés and I went to find Felipe and El Mono, and we rested for maybe ten or fifteen minutes and then we kept walking. By this time it was three or four in the afternoon. We kept walking and walking, but then it started to get dark and we had to stop. We were "downriver," that's what they call it. We got out a small tent we had and we washed our shirts, *la vaina* . . .

ME: Was that when Andrés cried?

JOHAN (*laughing*): No, that was before.

Not long after we met in Panama, Felipe had sent me a tranche of photos and videos of the journey thus far, including a short film of Andrés crying by a Darién river, which the others would never let him live down. There was footage of the four of them trudging up mountains wielding machetes and small backpacks, plus some images from Acandí the night before entering the jungle, among them a photo shoot series with a Buddhist monk in an orange robe, who had apparently remained serenely seated in a plastic chair while they took turns posing grinningly with him and flashing whatever hand signals are flashed these days.

JOHAN: We slept that night by the river—well in reality we couldn't even sleep because it was totally dark and you never know when the river is going to rise all of a sudden. You don't hear birds or anything in the selva even though it's a selva and you should hear birds *y vaina* but you don't hear anything, only sometimes at night you hear screams.

ME: Seriously?

JOHAN: Seriously. People scream in the night in the selva, maybe from all of the *muertos* they have seen in there; it's crazy. In the morning we got up at like five o'clock and waited for it to start getting light. We got up, *la vaina*, and we continued walking; we continued walking and walking. We crossed a ton of rivers, I don't know how many in reality but a lot, and then at eleven o'clock or noon we got to the *piraguas* [canoes used by Indigenous communities in the Darién]. You have to pay fifteen or twenty dollars for the piragua to take you to Bajo Chiquito, but we made a deal with the dudes to take us practically for free—we gave them some marijuana Andrés had from Colombia, and the dudes took us on the piragua and even gave us food. We got to Bajo Chiquito and we stayed there in the village that night, and from there you had to pay for another piragua, but we didn't have the money so we had to walk.

ME: And you didn't meet a gringa at some point?

JOHAN: Yes, in Bajo Chiquito we met la señora Belén . . .

ME: (*grumbles*)

JOHAN: We met la señorita Belén and we talked with her—well it was the other *pana* who did most of the talking. We met him in

Bajo Chiquito, too, but we got separated later in Mexico. They didn't want to let la señorita Belén into Bajo Chiquito because she was a journalist *y vaina*, but she got in anyway and she saw us cooking rice and was curious so she came and talked to us. And then she left and we continued on our way, but we stayed in touch with her. And we're still in touch with her (*laughs*).

Johan had by this time decided that he was not a fan of Spain and would rather go back to Venezuela, a decision the American in me told me I should be pissed about given the time and resources that had gone into his passport and transatlantic movement. The rest of me, however, was pleased that he had chosen his family over the prospect of a paycheck in euros—and also that he would be close by and potentially available to escort me into the Darién Gap if need be.

ME: So how was your experience in the Darién overall?

JOHAN (*following a long pause and a half-laugh*): Difficult. I mean, difficult because nothing is easy. But I was scared the whole time that an animal would attack us or someone would rob or kill us. We had our machetes obviously that we bought in Necoclí or Medellín in case we needed them for whatever *vaina*, but *gracias a Dios* nothing happened. But it was definitely an experience I won't forget.

ME: And was it worth it or no?

JOHAN: Of course it was worth it. Because we're alive. Because we're here.

ME: If you had to do it again would you?

JOHAN (*long pause*): I don't know. No . . . I don't know, but no, no . . .

ME: So you're not taking me to the Darién?

JOHAN: If you want me to of course I will, but I would just do it to protect you so nothing happens to you, since I more or less know what the deal is now. But for me to decide to cross the selva again to go to the U.S. traveling like we did, sleeping on the street and going through all the shit we went through, no.

ME: OK.

JOHAN: OK.

Later that very night it was decided, with the assistance of a good quantity of Venezuelan rum, that Johan would indeed accompany me into the jungle—a service for which he would be financially compensated—in January 2024, thus resolving the logistical dilemma of how I would enter the Darién Gap as neither a journalist nor a tourist. This gave me three and a half months to self-combust in pre-jungle panic, and Johan three and a half months to continually reassure me that God was with us. At some point over these months Johan's brother was enlisted to join the expedition as well, as I figured the more machetes the better.

And yet this would be only the second of three trips into the Gap for Johan, who contrary to his pledge to not endure shit to get to the United States again ended up doing just that in March of 2024. Although he had returned from Spain full of hope for his new life back home, his efforts to sell clothing and then food items at a market in Caracas had failed when he lacked sufficient funds to pay the police whatever sum they required to permit his commercial activity. Construction work had dried up after only a few days, his daughter needed new shoes, and U.S. sanctions only made everything in Venezuela all the more impossibly tedious— not to mention downright life-threatening; in 2017–18 alone, according to the Washington, D.C.–based Center for Economic and Policy Research, sanctions caused more than forty thousand deaths in the country. Anyone underestimating the deadly power of such coercive economic measures would do well to recall then–U.S. ambassador to the United Nations Madeleine Albright's upbeat assessment in 1996 regarding the estimate that half a million Iraqi children had been killed by U.S. sanctions: "We think the price is worth it."[23]

After observing that Andrés, Felipe, El Mono, and the other friends he had met on the road were all already precariously employed in the United States and sending money back to their families—the U.S. economy is, after all, dependent on undocumented and exploitable labor—Johan concluded that it was only logical for him to once again head north. The goal, as always, was simply to earn enough money to be able to return home.

Johan's story was not, to be sure, the most dramatic of migration tales. He was not fleeing political persecution, torture, or criminal gangs; life was just not economically sustainable. And so, like so many millions of other people have done over the years, he picked up and headed off in the direction of the country largely responsible for sustaining global systemic inequality, where, with the grace of God—as they say—he'd make enough to buy his kid new shoes and then some. His third and final Darién experience in March 2024 would be decidedly unlucky—even worse than the dream he'd had prior to his first trip—and was summed up in a WhatsApp message to me from Bajo Chiquito, where we had met almost exactly a year earlier: "Mi amor bello I'm alive, I came out of the jungle this morning gracias a Dios. I'm super destroyed. But I'm alive."

Which, in the end, is more than can be said for many of those who enter the jungle in search of a better life.

Flying into the Panamanian capital of Panama City, one descends over a teeming mass of skyscrapers set against the bay—a monument to money laundering that, at least from the air, serves to conceal the assorted slums and squalor below. It is a fittingly capitalist backdrop, no doubt, for a hemispheric crossroads where, as CNN apocalyptically warned its American audience in August 2023, a severe drought affecting the Panama Canal was "not a good sign for supply chains—or your holiday shopping."

I arrived in Panama from Mexico six months prior to the doomsday alert, in February 2023, for a two-week stay. The bulk of my visit was to be spent in the town of Metetí in Darién province, more than an hour's drive from the migrant camp in Bajo Chiquito where I would meet Johan. Although I already knew at this point that I would eventually need to actually enter the jungle rather than tiptoe around its edges, I had not yet grown the balls to do so and was still in reconnaissance mode.

It was my first trip to Panama in ten years, the last having transpired in 2013, when my mom and dad had taken up residence in one such Panama City skyscraper as part of my dad's short-lived experiment in recuperating his Canal Zone youth. My parents had then settled in Barcelona for almost eight years, before a pandemic-induced lapse in judgment and their first grandson had brought them back to the homeland. In Panama City I stayed with a Québécois friend—we'll call him Émile—who had offered to drive me to Metetí. I did not know him well, but as far as I could tell Émile had accumulated a small fortune on account of various international investments—among them casinos in the Mexican city of Monterrey—and generally attempted to compensate for his privilege by not behaving like a rich asshole. He would become a primary funder of the trans-American migration of Johan and his friends, whom my father would quickly take to calling the *Siete Magníficos*.

I met Émile in December 2009 on a flight from Panama City to Buenos Aires, Argentina, where my parents had initially moved from Texas after ostensibly coming to the same conclusion I had reached years before: that life was too short to spend any more of it in the United States. I had just completed four months in Honduras, where the June U.S.-endorsed coup against the ever so slightly left-leaning Manuel Zelaya had propelled violence and impunity to new heights, including a surge in femicides. Much of the criminal behavior was perpetrated by Honduran forces of law and order on the receiving end of U.S. funds and other assistance—just like in the good old Cold War days of Battalion 316, described in a 1995 *Baltimore Sun* article as the "CIA-trained military unit that terrorized Honduras for much of the 1980s."[24] Then as now, the U.S. mission was to make the world safe for capitalist pillage, and, to that end, the slogan of the right-wing post-coup regime was "Honduras Is Open for Business"—not that it ever wasn't.

Hardly a socialist, Zelaya had merely committed the unpardonable crime of daring to steer the country from the straight and narrow path of neoliberal dystopia with a few cosmetic adjustments to business as usual. Among these was the idea that poverty-stricken Honduran communities whose land was being thoroughly contaminated by international corporate mining projects should perhaps be consulted about the whole arrangement. Then there was the matter of raising the monthly urban and rural minimum wages to $290 and $213, respectively, which was far too much for the oppressed Honduran oligarchs to bear.

Of course, you can't overthrow a president just for giving people the opportunity to be a little less fantastically poor, so Zelaya was instead accused of conspiring to remain president of Honduras in violation of the constitutional one-term limit—a demonstrably false claim that nonetheless saw him carted off to Costa Rica in his pajamas one fine June morning by the Honduran military, and that was the end of that. Six years later, in 2015, this same constitutional term limit was summarily dispensed with in order to pave the way for the continued rule of U.S. buddy Juan Orlando Hernández, whose homicidal security forces duly "terrorized Honduras," to borrow the *Baltimore Sun*'s earlier words. After recognizing Hernández's 2017 reelection despite sweeping fraud allegations, the United States spontaneously demoted the man from his role as a prized ally in the so-called war on drugs to his new function as the empire's latest narco-nemesis, and in March 2024 he was convicted in a Manhattan federal court on three counts of drug trafficking and weapons conspiracy.

The schizophrenic imperial switcheroo was, it so happens, reminiscent of the fate that had befallen the leader of another Central American territory traditionally regarded by the United States as its own private military base. A longtime U.S. chum and the de facto ruler of Panama from 1983 until 1989, Manuel Noriega was swiftly converted into the face of evil and hauled up to Miami in 1990 to face drug-trafficking and other charges, receiving a forty-year sentence in 1992. Never mind that the very same Noriega had spent decades on the CIA payroll notwithstanding full U.S. awareness, since at least 1972, of his involvement in drug trafficking—a business the United States had long been up to its ears in anyway, as evidenced by, inter alia, the December 1993 *New York Times* headline, "The CIA Drug Connection Is as Old as the Agency."

On January 3, 1990, Noriega surrendered to his former gringo friends after his brief stay at the Vatican embassy in Panama City was interrupted by the U.S. tanks parked outside, which treated him to a carefully selected rotation of musical torture, including

Bon Jovi's "Wanted Dead or Alive" and Lee Greenwood's "God Bless the U.S.A." A few weeks later, on January 23, the *Los Angeles Times* would report that "the 50 pounds of cocaine U.S. officials said they found last month in a house used by ousted Gen. Manuel A. Noriega turned out to be tamales wrapped in banana leaves, the Pentagon admitted today." U.S. Southern Command (SOUTHCOM) chief General Maxwell Thurman had "repeated the allegation, only raising the 'cocaine' cache's weight to 110 pounds," while Defense Department spokeswoman Major Kathy Wood appeared to caution against overestimating the innocence of the tamal: "It's a bonding material. . . . It's a substance they used in voodoo rituals."[25]

As the prelude to Noriega's extradition, on December 20, 1989, the U.S. military had set about bombing the living daylights out of the impoverished Panama City neighborhood of El Chorrillo, a particularly flammable area given the prevalence of wooden shacks that had once housed the workers who built the Panama Canal. Bodies were flung into mass graves, and fatality estimates ranged from a few hundred to several thousand, depending on whether you asked the United States or human rights organizations. At any rate, the destruction was sufficient to earn El Chorrillo the temporary moniker "Little Hiroshima," while the U.S. establishment once again flaunted its infinite capacity for sick irony by dubbing the expedited assault on Panama "Operation Just Cause." Although then–U.S. secretary of defense Dick Cheney would subsequently brag that Just Cause had "been the most surgical military operation of its size ever conducted," you can't really have a surgical Hiroshima.[26] More than five thousand refugees from the carnage would be temporarily housed at Balboa High School, my dad's former stomping grounds.

Underscoring the categorically unjust nature of the cause was the fact that Noriega's overthrow was overseen by President George H. W. Bush—the same character who as director of the CIA in 1976 had ensured the soon-to-be Panamanian dictator's preservation on the agency payroll and as vice president in 1981 had renewed cooperation. The largest U.S. combat operation since the Vietnam War, the quick-and-easy victory in Panama was intended to curb that pesky domestic affliction known as Vietnam Syndrome and serve as a practice run for Bush's impending war on Iraq: Operation Desert Storm, launched in 1991.

In both Just Cause and Desert Storm, flashy air power proved a key combat selling point, as television-glued Americans quickly revealed a soft spot for video game–style blow-'em-up spectacles— pardon, "surgical military operations." Even U.S. general Marc Cisneros—an "overlooked hero" of Just Cause, as per the *Tampa Bay Times*—candidly admitted on the tenth anniversary of the operation in 1999: "I think we could have done it with less troops and less destruction. We made it look like we were battling Goliath." Cisneros went on to muse, "We are mesmerized with firepower. We have all these new gadgets, laser-guided missiles and stealth fighters, and we are just dying to use that stuff."[27] As for the folks doing the literal dying, the Inter-American Commission on Human Rights ruled in 2018 that the United States should "provide full reparation for the human rights violations" committed during the military invasion of Panama, "including both the material and moral dimensions."[28] One guess how all of that has panned out.

The invasion was meanwhile naturally facilitated by the fact that the United States had saturated Panamanian territory with military installations, rendering it a sort of invasion-from-within and further underscoring the United States' utter disdain for any borders aside from its own. Indeed, it was nearly impossible to maneuver within the former Canal Zone without tripping over one military base or another, a landscape only befitting a nation that was itself "Made in the USA," as John Weeks and Phil Gunson put it in their 1991 book *Panama*—"a country carved out of the heart of Latin America to serve the objectives of a foreign power."[29] The carving had taken place when it was deemed to be easier than negotiating the proposed canal zone with Colombia, to which Panama belonged until 1903. In 1902 a Dr. José Vicente Concha, one of the Colombian diplomats involved in failed negotiations in Washington, wrote presciently of his American counterparts: "The desire to make themselves appear, as a Nation, most respectful of the rights of others forces these gentlemen to toy a little with their prey before devouring it, although when all is said and done, they will do so in one way or other."[30] In *The Path Between the Seas*, McCullough writes that Concha "suffered a physical and emotional collapse upon resigning his post and reportedly was put on a ship in New York in a strait jacket."[31]

In the Canal Zone the United States had presided over a system of racial segregation that would persist even after such things became uncool in the United States itself—think whites-only drinking fountains, segregated schools, and so forth. Notes McCullough: "Whenever a mosquito was seen in a white household, the Sanitary Department was notified and immediately a black man came with chloroform and a glass vial to catch the insect and take it back to the laboratory for analysis."[32] From 1946 until 1984, imperial infrastructure in Panama would also comprise the U.S. Army School of the Americas, attended by many a regional dictator and death squad leader, including Argentina's Jorge Rafael Videla, El Salvador's Roberto d'Aubuisson, and Manuel Noriega himself, whose unceremonious removal to Miami would predictably do nothing for the "war on drugs." As Noam Chomsky has written: "The US put the bankers back in power after the invasion. Noriega's involvement in drug trafficking had been trivial compared to theirs."[33]

In the wee hours of December 20, just as Just Cause was kicking off, Noriega's chosen successor Guillermo Endara was sworn in as president of Panama in a secretive ceremony at Fort Clayton, the army base where he had been summoned by SOUTHCOM. Like Albrook Air Force Station, Howard Air Force Base, and other pillars of the U.S. occupation of Panama, Fort Clayton was named for a U.S. military officer whose memory has been preserved in Panamanian geography in the post-occupation era. Clayton is now an upscale residential area catering to the "expat" crowd and NGO types, while Albrook refers to a mall located on none other than Roosevelt Avenue—an ode to the man who carved Panama out of Latin America's heart. For its part, Fourth of July Avenue was eventually renamed Martyrs' Avenue in honor of the victims of the 1964 flag riots.

Operation Just Cause was coordinated from Quarry Heights Military Reservation on Ancón Hill, the Southern Command headquarters that owed its name to the hillside rock quarry that had been exploited for canal construction. And it was in the Quarry Heights neighborhood—now sans U.S. military reservation—that I was hosted in Émile's most unshabby abode prior to departing for Meletí. By great coincidence, Émile's guest room offered a direct view of my grandparents' sprawling former residence some few hundred meters away, which they had inhabited during my grandfather's stint in the 1970s as SOUTHCOM's director of military intelligence. His Panamanian counterpart at the time was the one and only Manuel Noriega, who prior to assuming leadership of the country served as director of military intelligence under appointed "Maximum Leader of the Revolution" Omar Torrijos. My granddad, known to friends and family as "the Colonel," had entered the world in Tampa, Florida, the only son of poor Spanish immigrants— José and Flora—who reached the United States via Havana and whose domestic habits in Tampa were recorded by my dad in one of various unpublished memoirs: "Even though the house was tied into the city sewage system, José was convinced that using the toilet was not good for the plumbing. On occasion a visitor would catch Flora, skirt lifted away from her legs, peeing in a Bustelo Cuban coffee can, whose contents were later dumped in the yard."

On paper, then, the Colonel appeared to embody the American dream, rising from a monolingual Spanish immigrant household that urinated in Café Bustelo cans to a decorated military career that encompassed the D-Day landing at Normandy, the Korean and Vietnam Wars, and a briefing of U.S. defense secretary Robert McNamara during the Cuban Missile Crisis. My granddad's role as imperial emissary had, however, failed to instill in him the proper ideological coherence, and he expressed intermittent sympathy for Che Guevara and the Viet Cong. Compounded by a lifetime of dedicated alcohol consumption, his wartime pursuits would come back to haunt him at the end of his years, when he could be seen racing nude through the corridors of his Texas nursing home or phoning his children from under the bed to report that the Russians were attacking and that he would notify them when the coast was clear. He died in 2003, the same year I graduated from Columbia University in New York and undertook to exile myself from the country.

While on SOUTHCOM duty in the Canal Zone, the Colonel attended regular meetings with Noriega in a bunker on Ancón Hill known as the Tunnel. Now sealed off, the Tunnel reportedly remains air-conditioned to this day, an appropriately tragicomic colonial vestige and testament to the general futility of the universe. My first activity upon arriving at Émile's place in Quarry Heights was to stage the obligatory trek up Ancón Hill, in gratifyingly overpowering humidity, for the view of skyscrapers and canal, pausing at the entrance to the hillside bunker for a visceral and fleeting moment of guilty vicarious nostalgia.

The next activity was to accompany Émile to a dinner engagement with a fellow Canadian, "Derek," who unlike Émile spoke no Spanish despite having lived in Panama for no fewer than twelve years and who worked in the international mining sector—an iniquitous Canadian-heavy industry that makes a rather fine mockery of the country's claims to be merely the United States' innocent northern neighbor. A caricature of the first-world expatriate who descends upon the Global South to inhabit a neocolonial bubble, Derek was an updated version of the "Zonian," the pseudo-ethnic denomination for a U.S. citizen from the Canal Zone—many of whom were also linguistically challenged when it came to Spanish but masters of the hubris that usually attends the conquest of other people's land. Émile, being fully aware of my own worldviews, had optimistically decided that my inclusion in the dinner could be amusing.

From Quarry Heights Émile and I were dispatched to fetch Derek from his place of residence: a waterfront luxury condo in what was formerly branded the Trump Ocean Club International Hotel and Tower and is still locally referred to as "the Trump," although the then-president's surname was eliminated from the tower's sign with a hammer and crowbar in 2018. The previous year, NBC News reported that The Trump Organization had licensed its name to the seventy-story eyesore "riddled with ties to drug money and international organized crime."[34] On the drive to the Trump, Émile introduced me to the music video of the just-released single *Yo Soy El Guru* ("I Am the Guru"), starring sep-tuagenarian former Panamanian president Ricardo Martinelli in collaboration with the Panamanian rapper DJ Black and various bikini-clad women in a boat off Panama City. The spectacle was apparently intended to boost the right-wing Martinelli's chances of reprising his presidency in 2024, but a wrench was thrown in the works in July 2023 when a Panamanian judge had the nerve to sentence *El Guru* to ten and a half years in prison for money laundering.

The evening got off to an encouraging start when I had to don my sweater and 2-meter-long winter scarf in the car in order to accommodate Derek's required A/C levels. It was then Derek's turn for acute discomfort when Émile, discovering that his friend had not once in a dozen years in Panama set foot in El Chorrillo, decided to take us for a pre-dinner spin through the neighborhood amid Derek's protests that surely nonresidents of the area were banned from entering. We survived the viewing of poor people and anti-American graffiti in remembrance of Just Cause and emerged unscathed back into the bubble for a feast at a restaurant suitable for a tenant of the Trump. Émile and I discussed our next-morning departure for Metetí—where Émile would deposit me and return to Panama City—and Derek contributed relevant details about past and upcoming vacations on Caribbean islands.

As usual, I had not made any specific journalistic plans for the Darién, partly out of laziness and partly on account of my almost-neurotic aversion to behaving like a normal journalist. I had managed to contact Doctors Without Borders (*Médecins Sans Frontières* or MSF), an organization I had long ago diagnosed as being far less irritating than other NGOs and that had assisted me with previous stories on Syrian refugees in Lebanon and Eritrean refugees in Italy. MSF maintained an office in Meterí and advised me that I would need Panamanian government permission in order to visit the migrant reception stations of San Vicente and Lajas Blancas, where MSF also provided services. Migrants were transferred to these reception stations following initial processing at the Indigenous villages of Bajo Chiquito and Canaan Membrillo, the two points of arrival from the jungle; from San Vicente and Lajas Blancas, they were loaded onto buses bound for the Costa Rican border. I would additionally need permission for any sort of incursion into the Darién Gap itself, and MSF provided me with the contact information for the person at Panama's Ministry of Public Security who was in charge of ruling on such matters.

Having never been in possession of any sort of press credentials, I figured I might as well try my luck and dashed off a chipper WhatsApp message to the Public Security person. Left on read, I set about googling adventure tour operators in Panama that specialized in Darién jungle expeditions in order to inquire about the possibility of procuring a jungle entrance permit without actually having to participate in a tour—enticing as they all sounded. One company, for example, offered three days in the "mysterious" Darién Gap under the supervision of "passionate Embera tribe guides." The company website featured the following trip description, helpfully translated for the benefit of the adventurous Anglophone:

> It is a forgotten place, a savage place that shows us the best and worst in us all. The dense jungle topography of the Darien Gap has long been the disastrous end of many adventurers, swallowing lost souls in its ancient embrace. The aura of the jungle, of a million wild souls, is as tangible as water when one bathes. . . .

Both ambitious human aspirations and ultimate despair cross paths in this mystical place, drawing all manner of people into its grasp. Trafficked by merciless smugglers and hopeful migrants alike, the Darien Gap has seen and claimed countless of travelers, while only a few lucky ones were given the privilege to escape its dark fangs.

The fangs were not so much of an issue for the package tourist, of course, and prospective expedition participants were assured: "The sound of nature is a symphony unlike another. Its music will lull you to sleep as you lie comfortably in your bed, in the middle of the jungle."[35] I emailed the company with a made-up story about how I had promised my dead grandfather that I would make a pilgrimage to the Darién Gap and could I just pay them to obtain whatever paper I needed to pop in and out of the jungle; the response was quick and negative, and I was politely informed that tourists were not permitted to circulate in the area without the company of a guide due to incidents of "lost, drowned, and disappeared travelers." That having been settled, I reverted to my usual journalistic approach, which was to just screw it all and see what happened.

Derek was not overly aware of the goings-on in the Darién Gap but speculated that whatever the crisis was, it was surely the fault of leftist governments. By the end of dinner Émile and I had however heard about such actual real-life emergencies as the time the air-conditioning went out in the Trump and Derek had to open his window. Redepositing Derek in his waterfront tower, Émile and I returned to Quarry Heights—the former command center of the U.S. occupation of a made-in-USA nation—and set out in the morning for the Darién, site of an ongoing made-in-USA migration crisis. Accompanying us on the five-hour drive was a female Panamanian friend of Émile's who had previously also lived in Quarry Heights—in the house formerly inhabited by Operation Just Cause hero general Marc Cisneros, no less—and who had never been to Darién province.

Leaving the skyscrapers behind, it was a straight shot down the Pan-American Highway, which did not consistently live up to its grandiose title and was at times reduced to potholes and dust. On the border separating the provinces of Panamá and Darién, we were waved through the checkpoint operated by Panama's National Border Service, known by its Spanish acronym SENAFRONT (*Servicio Nacional de Fronteras*). Panama has no army, as the institution was abolished for the second time in the nation's history following the 1989 invasion, but the camouflage-clad SENAFRONT folks make a fine visual substitute. When I later returned by bus to Panama City, I was briefly removed from the vehicle at this same checkpoint and sent over to a special booth to sign out of the Darién, as it were, despite never having signed in. The only other foreigners on the bus, four Chinese men, were removed permanently and presumably sent back to a migrant reception station to board the migrant-specific bus to Costa Rica, which was the only means of transport the Panamanian government had authorized for its guests in transit. At the time, the government was charging migrants forty dollars per person for this service, though the fee was later raised to sixty dollars—that is, far pricier than the regular bus, in keeping with the cruel logic of the contemporary migration industry: that people who are often on the move precisely because they don't have money should be charged more for everything. Just prior to my arrival in Panama, one such Costa Rica–bound bus had crashed in the province of Chiriquí, killing forty-one migrants on board.

Since no road trip to Darién was complete without a visit to the end of the road, Émile drove us forty-five minutes past Metetí to the old Spanish frontier post of Yaviza—now the last stop in Panama before the Pan-American Highway gives way to the Darién Gap, picking up again on the other side in Colombia. The obligatory photographs were taken by the "Bienvenidos a Yaviza" sign, which stipulated that we were 12,580 kilometers from the highway's starting point in Alaska. Contrary to dramatic expectations, we did not find ourselves suddenly face-to-face with the "dark fangs" of the mythical Gap; rather, we found ourselves in the middle of Yaviza's Carnival festivities, which consisted of a few dozen revelers being sprayed with a high-pressure hose while music blasted from a loudspeaker.

Not far from the hubbub was a SENAFRONT officer positioned next to a list of prohibited items including guns, coolers, and nail clippers. He shrugged when I asked about the clippers, offering only the assessment that *el panameño cuando toma es un problema*—"when Panamanians drink it's a problem." Migrants were hardly ever seen these days in Yaviza, he said, although I would later learn that migrant corpses did periodically turn up after floating down the Chucunaque River, which flowed through the town. On the day of our visit, the river was calm, boasting an assortment of piraguas filled with bananas and a large collection of trash on its banks.

Speaking of migrant corpses and trash, just a few weeks earlier, on January 31, the body of a young Venezuelan man identified as José Luis Parejas Caraballo had been found in a Darién garbage truck. As per the report in Panama's *El Siglo* newspaper, the young man had arrived January 28 in Bajo Chiquito from the jungle and was transferred to the migrant reception station at Lajas Blancas. This was the last place he was seen before being discovered lifeless among the refuse as a garbage truck belonging to the Marvez company was emptied at the "La Milagrosa" dump near Metetí. According to the truck's driver, he had made his usual morning garbage collection rounds and then stopped for an hour's lunch, leaving the vehicle parked on the side of the Pan-American Highway; the next thing he knew, a waste picker at La Milagrosa was alerting him to the presence of a cadaver dangling from the back of his truck.[36]

As I would soon hear in Metetí, the rumor was that there had been no foul play and that Parejas Caraballo had simply stowed away in the garbage truck as a means of escaping Lajas Blancas, where conditions were notoriously grisly. The driver's extended roadside lunch break in the baking sun and humidity had presumably only accelerated the man's asphyxiation, and he had arrived at La Milagrosa dead. A photograph had circulated on Metetí cell phones of Parejas Caraballo's body, hanging upside down in a black Nike T-shirt with his hands over his head and surrounded by plastic bags, water bottles, and Styrofoam food containers. While the image was no doubt suitably symbolic of the negligible value assigned to migrant lives, its propagation by cell phone almost felt like a violation in itself. A few days into my stay in Metetí, another photograph would fuel renewed morbid migrant gossip when an unidentified man hanged himself from a tree near Lajas Blancas. Presumed to be Venezuelan, as well, the young man had apparently survived the jungle only to take his own life.

Avoiding the Carnival hose in Yaviza, we got back in Émile's car for the short drive to Metetí, where I was dropped at a hotel called Hospedaje Aruba and Émile and his friend returned to Panama City. The Aruba was run by Chinese immigrants to Panama, as were the shops on either side of it; down the street was an evangelical church where the pastor specialized in shouting himself hoarse. In a testament to the intensity of the Darién climate, even I was forced to intermittently turn on the A/C in my hotel room, a process that required balancing precariously on a chair while risking electrocution.

As luck would have it, I got to spend my first full day in Metetí stuck in said room writing an article for *Al Jazeera* on the Chinese "spy balloon" that had recently been downed by a U.S. fighter jet off the coast of South Carolina. Energized by the balloon's demise, the U.S. military had then gone about frenziedly blowing up more unidentified items in the sky—one of which, according to *Aviation Week*, may have been a cheap balloon reported missing by the Northern Illinois Bottlecap Balloon Brigade, a hobbyist club. China's top diplomat, Wang Yi, had urged the U.S. government "not to do such preposterous things simply to divert attention from its own domestic problems"—fair enough advice given the country's surplus of terrestrial issues, ranging from the homelessness epidemic to the fact that mass shootings might as well be declared an official national pastime.[37] Then, of course, there's the matter of illegal mass domestic surveillance, which occurs on a level no "spy balloon" could ever aspire to, and the government's preference for spending money on blowing things up rather than on food, education, housing, or health care. The Sidewinder missiles utilized to vanquish the Chinese balloon and the other unidentified objects, for instance, came at $400,000 a pop.

Once I had submitted my thoughts on the balloon, I was free to explore. My first destination after the grocery store was San Vicente, the migrant reception station where Trumpite Laura Loomer would do battle the following year with busloads of "invaders from Africa." A short minibus ride from the Aruba, San Vicente had somehow come to be known by Spanish-speaking migrants as *la ONU*—the Spanish acronym for the United Nations—as had the other migrant reception station at Lajas Blancas, despite neither being a U.N. installation. When I arrived around midday, three large buses full of migrants were lined up out front, ready to depart for Costa Rica. My attempt to simply stroll past the SENAFRONT official stationed at the entrance to the camp was immediately thwarted, and I was informed that— whether or not it was true that I had an appointment with the MSF team inside—I was not going a step further without the proper permission from Panama City. Furthermore, the guard told me, I should look into getting myself an umbrella if I was going to be traipsing around under the scorching sun.

Inaugurated in September 2020 with a capacity of five hundred persons, San Vicente was typically the stopping point for migrants who had exited the jungle at the Indigenous village of Canaan Membrillo, where they were sent by piragua to Puerto Limón and then bused to the camp. By contrast, those arriving at Bajo Chiquito were sent by piragua to Lajas Blancas. In some cases, migrants were able to evade the reception stations; Johan and his friends, for example, sneaked from Bajo Chiquito to Metetí and boarded a bus to Panama City, from which they were promptly removed at the SENAFRONT checkpoint. They eventually reached the city via a combination of walking and hitchhiking and from there continued by bus to the Costa Rican border. As Johan put it to me: "We didn't go in *la ONU* because we met a guy who told us it was crazy in there, that there were too many people *y vaina* and that if we went in we would leave there fucked up."

Indeed, news out of San Vicente and Lajas Blancas did little to inspire confidence. Earlier in February, the Spanish daily *El País* had exposed the highlights of an as yet unpublished report by the actual *ONU*—specifically the United Nations Special Rapporteur on the human rights of migrants—according to which migrants in Panama were suffering sexual and other abuses at the hands of SENAFRONT and Panamanian immigration personnel. Among the alleged abuses was the solicitation of sexual favors from migrant women and girls in exchange for promises of free transport to Costa Rica. Forced labor was also reported in San Vicente and Lajas Blancas, "deplorable and unsanitary" places where migrants were effectively "deprived of liberty," with some families being detained for more than three months. The U.N. warned that the conditions in the camps could qualify as "cruel, inhuman or degrading treatment" and could give rise to "violations of the right to life and personal integrity."[38] For its part, the Panamanian government had issued a huffy rejection of the international effort to "undermine the humanitarian labor" being nobly carried out by the selfless representatives of the Panamanian state.[39]

Thwarted from viewing for myself the humanitarian labor underway at San Vicente, I waited on the side of the Pan-American Highway for the minibus back to the Aruba, which did not materialize, causing me to think that perhaps the SENAFRONT official had been right about the sun umbrella. I finally flagged down a taxi, whose middle-aged driver agreed to drop me at the Aruba for two dollars. Normally a bus driver for the Darién campus of the University of Panama, Belisario drove the taxi in his spare time. His nephew had also been a taxi driver, he told me, before he was jailed indefinitely for migrant smuggling—which was why

Belisario himself now had to be careful about whom he picked up. In Belisario's version of the story, his nephew had been approached by an undercover agent posing as a migrant, who offered him $200 for a ride to Panama City. And while the Panamanian government enjoys bleating about its ostensible successes in cracking down on smuggling operations—among other "humanitarian labor"—it's not so much a crackdown as a maintenance of a state monopoly on the smuggling business. After all, charging persons whom the state considers illegally present in Panamanian territory a fee to transport them to another border for the purpose of "illegal" crossing fits the definition of migrant smuggling rather well.

The United States, of course, is forever harping on about the need to crack down on migration through the Darién, and on February 14 a meeting between U.S., Panamanian, and Colombian officials had taken place in Colombia in order to "better understand the challenges of collaborative migration management," as per the press release from the U.S. embassy in Bogotá. Following a fly-over of the area around a joint Colombian-Panamanian security base on the border, "the three sides committed to close coordination." The press release emphasized that the United States continued to "combat illegal human smuggling and trafficking operations that promote and facilitate the dangerous crossing through the Darien Gap"—operations that wouldn't exist, mind you, if the United States did not insist on wreaking global havoc while simultaneously criminalizing migration.[40]

In April of 2023, the same three countries announced the kickoff of a sixty-day effort to halt migration through the Darién Gap, and in June Panama launched two initiatives—the "Shield" campaign and "Operation Chocó"—aimed at tackling organized crime, securing Panama's borders, and stopping and deporting migrants, all with the help of U.S.-donated helicopters. "Preserv[ing] the vital rainforest" was also a stated goal, as though the petty litter generated by migrants was somehow worse than, I dunno, the first-world industrial pollution and general environmental devastation driving the planet's rapid self-combustion—itself a key factor fueling mass migration in the first place. On the ground, however, little discernible headway was made, and more than 520,000 people crossed the Darién Gap in 2023. The following May, the U.N. estimated that 800,000 migrants would traverse the jungle in 2024, including 160,000 children and adolescents. In the first four months of the year alone, some 30,000 children made the crossing—a 40 percent increase over 2023, according to the U.N. Children's Fund (UNICEF). Of these 30,000 children, UNICEF calculated, nearly 2,000 of them were "unaccompanied or separated from their families," while the number of children transiting the Gap was "growing five-times faster than the number of adults."

In September 2023, just after a record 81,946 people had reportedly crossed the Darién Gap in August, 77 percent of them Venezuelan, Colombia's leftist president Gustavo Petro complained about the United States' nonsolution to the crisis in the *Tapón del Darién*—literally the "Darién Plug," as it's known in Spanish. The U.S.-backed approach, Petro stated, was to *taponar el Tapón*—plug the Plug—which in addition to being "quite difficult" would also be ineffective. A more efficient move, he suggested, would involve removing U.S. sanctions on Venezuela—a no-brainer in theory, but only if one assumes that the U.S. goal in the region is in fact to ease human suffering rather than to exacerbate crises in order to justify further hemispheric militarization and related imperial schemes. The idea to *taponar el Tapón* would resurface in May 2024 with the victory in the Panamanian presidential election of José Raúl Mulino, the stand-in for Ricardo "*El Guru*" Martinelli, who promised to shut down the Darién Gap. In reality, this was about as feasible as shutting down the Mediterranean Sea—another migration route where concerned governments like to pretend that traffickers and smugglers are the entire problem. Meanwhile, Panama continued to enthusiastically welcome other types of travelers, and in July 2024 the mayor of Panama City would offer tourists affected by Barcelona's anti-tourism protests an all-expenses-paid vacation in his own country.

According to the International Crisis Group, an estimated ninety-seven different nationalities crossed the Darién Gap in the first seven months of 2023; the vast majority of migrants were Venezuelan, followed by Haitians and Ecuadoreans. Cubans were no longer a fixture in the jungle, owing to Nicaragua's decision in November 2021 to lift visa requirements for citizens of the island nation, allowing them to circumvent the Gap by flying to Nicaragua—an opportunity that my Cuban interlocutors in jail in Tapachula had missed by five months. In the taxi on the way to the Aruba, Belisario informed me that there had been a brief flurry of movement through the Darién Gap in the opposite direction in October 2022 in response to a rumor that the United States had officially closed its land border to citizens of Venezuela.

On October 12, the U.S. Department of Homeland Security had announced a "new migration enforcement process for Venezuelans," which stipulated that "Venezuelans who enter the United States between ports of entry, without authorization, will be returned to Mexico." In other words, it was simply the United States' latest nonchalant violation of the human right to seek asylum as enshrined in the Universal Declaration of Human Rights, and the Biden administration's latest channeling of Trump on the border. In exchange for the Venezuelan semi-ban, which was later expanded to include citizens of Cuba, Haiti, and Nicaragua, up to twenty-four thousand Venezuelans per month were eligible for two-year "humanitarian" visas through a sponsorship program that would enable them to fly directly to the United States. Not long after the ban was announced, Belisario had met three young Venezuelan men at the bus station in Metetí; having made it all the way to Mexico, they had turned around and were now making their way back. He had driven them to Lajas Blancas to face the jungle once again, and explained that since they were traveling away from the U.S. border and not toward it, there was no danger of him being busted for migrant smuggling in this case. The illusory success of U.S. deterrence strategy was predictably short-lived, and, following a momentary decrease in Venezuelans crossing the Darién Gap, numbers were now once again on the rise.

Belisario lived in Metetí with his wife and two sons, one of whom was a local calf-roping star. His daughter studied nursing in Panama City. As we passed a succession of migrant-packed buses that had departed Lajas Blancas for Costa Rica, Belisario shook his head and remarked that it was a shame everyone thought life in America was so great when there were people living under bridges. The plan to drop me at the Aruba was derailed when Belisario revealed that he was friends with a Venezuelan couple who had managed to escape San Vicente and were temporarily living in Metetí, a decidedly rare phenomenon. The husband was working at a carwash to scrape together funds for the onward journey, which is how Belisario had met him. He was not difficult to track down.

Jesús was thirty-three years old and hailed from the Venezuelan state of Falcón west of Caracas. Dressed in shorts, a wifebeater, and mirrored sunglasses, he leaned through Belisario's window to speak with us. He had crossed the Darién Gap from Capurganá with his wife and two-year-old son shortly after the implementation of the would-be Venezuelan ban; for most of the journey, which had taken them ten days, he had carried his son on his back. They had traveled with a group of approximately fifty people including Haitians, Indians, Arabs, and Chinese, and had been robbed by Indigenous assailants on the Panamanian side of the Gap, who also took their food and dumped it out. The taking of the food had, it seemed, constituted the gravest affront to his dignity in Jesús's eyes. Months had passed, and he could still not make sense of the act.

It had rained consistently in the jungle, which had slowed the group's progress. As they were descending the notorious *Loma de la Muerte* ("hill of death"), Jesús told Belisario and me, he had slipped and had begun to tumble down what had become a near-vertical slope of mud. Frantically grabbing hold of what he thought was a tree root, he quickly discovered that it was in fact a hand protruding from the mud and belonging to a human corpse. "I didn't tell my wife," he said. "But I thought to myself, 'That hand saved my life.'"

A snake had also made an appearance on the *Loma de la Muerte*. Jesús's wife Guailis would tell me when I spoke to her three days later that the hill itself reeked of death; on the ascent they had encountered an old man curled up dead beneath a tree "like he was cold," while on the hilltop they found a newly dead man and woman. The trek did a number on Jesús's feet, and by the time they got to San Vicente he could not walk. As soon as he could, the family made a break for it in the wee hours of the morning, slipping past SENAFRONT and immigration officials into relative freedom, whereupon they rented a shack on the side of the Pan-American Highway and Jesús went about looking for work. As Jesús described it, San Vicente was "no place for children," and the food and water provided to the migrants appeared to be linked to rampant stomach illnesses in the camp. His son had survived ten days in the jungle just fine, consuming water from the river, but in San Vicente had been immediately struck with a nasty case of diarrhea that lasted for five days. The situation was not helped by the single diaper the family had to their name.

Jesús and Guailis were not aiming for any particular destination in the United States; anywhere in the country would do. In the meantime, a portion of Jesús's meager earnings at the car wash were being sent to his mother in Venezuela, who was caring for his other four children. When we had finished chatting I gave him some money—and would later give Guailis more—which while not proper journalistic practice, I felt was only fair compensation for making people recount their plight to some gringa who had parachuted in on privilege. Belisario also helped the couple out when he could and had taken them *arroz con pollo* on New Year's.

Belisario and I would become friends, too, and he and his wife would subsequently accompany me on my unauthorized incursion into Bajo Chiquito. Meanwhile on February 21, the same day I spoke with Jesús, the Biden administration unveiled what would quickly be termed the U.S. "asylum ban"—this one for the benefit of all nationalities and not just Cubans, Haitians, Nicaraguans, and Venezuelans. The new rule was proposed in anticipation of the upsurge in arrivals to the U.S.-Mexico border that was predicted to follow the expiration in May of Title 42, the Trump-era policy that allowed the United States to summarily expel asylum seekers using the pandemic as a pretext.

Biden's version would largely eliminate the possibility of asylum for "individuals who circumvent available, established pathways to lawful migration . . . and also fail to seek protection in a country through which they traveled" before reaching the United States, as per the Department of Homeland Security communiqué.[41] In addition to contravening both U.S. and international law, the scheme presupposed that it is a piece of cake to "seek protection" in any old place on the way to the U.S. border—like, say, Honduras or Guatemala, both of which generate large numbers of asylum seekers themselves precisely because they are terrifically unsafe. As ever, the United States has an outsized hand in ensuring they remain so, while insufficient "pathways to lawful migration" force hundreds of thousands down the Darién path—where, if you're lucky, the hand of a mud-buried corpse just might save your life.

"Of course they didn't let you in; you look like a tourist."

This was the assessment offered by Tamara Guillermo, field coordinator for Doctors Without Borders (*Médecins Sans Frontières* or MSF) in Metetí, upon learning that I had been turned away from San Vicente earlier in the day. My wardrobe infractions were numerous: the shorts, the sunglasses, the several dozen bracelets that lined my arms and to which I had developed a pathological attachment. In fact, the bracelets had only been removed once in recent history, at the Siglo XXI detention center in Tapachula in 2021, a lengthy and traumatic process that had required the help of two policewomen. If I now wanted any chance of entering the Lajas Blancas migrant reception station undetected, Tamara scolded me, I had better revise my appearance.

It was my first of several hours-long meetings with Tamara, a no-nonsense and passionate Argentine who was initially unimpressed with my general lack of preparedness or my excuse that I was not a real journalist, just an opinion writer. I would gradually earn her approval—and even a series of clapping-hand emojis after I got into the migrant camp at Bajo Chiquito—but for the moment I resigned myself to the conclusion that I was utterly useless and resolved to do better.

MSF had operated in the Darién since April 2021, providing medical and psychological services to people on the move, and maintained a presence in both the San Vicente and Lajas

Blancas migrant reception stations. Prior to being posted to Metetí, Tamara had worked in Haiti, Ukraine, and Congo and reported that the "frightening" physical and mental state in which many refuge seekers arrived in Panama was unlike anything she had witnessed on other missions. Although she had given this same speech to journalists a million times before, she said, it never failed to move her, which became clear as she choked up various times recounting the "level of brutality" that had prompted Hispanophone migrants to christen the jungle *el infierno verde*—"the green hell."

Declaring the quantity of cadavers in the selva "immeasurable," Tamara enumerated the myriad causes of individual demise, ranging from heart attacks and drownings to decapitation by machete. In one case, a group of migrants had described the beheading of a one-year-old baby by a machete-wielding assailant who had warned the group that, if they didn't put a stop to the child's incessant crying, he would. As for the jungle's other infant casualties, Johan would tell me of a Haitian baby who had tumbled out of his mother's arms and over a precipice into a ravine—at which point his mother had endeavored to throw herself over the edge as well but was stopped from doing so by her companion.

Then, of course, there was the psychological impact on migrants of having to step over decomposing bodies; one Brazilian refuge seeker, for example, had spoken to MSF about the disconcerting effects of stumbling upon a dead person who had clearly been anally raped. When a Venezuelan woman in Mexico later recapped to me her own family's navigation of corpses in the Darién Gap—"I can say that we have all stepped on dead people"—it was done with a mixture of ironic fatalism, relief that *gracias a Dios* they themselves had not ended up trampled-upon cadavers, and guilt at having perhaps unwillingly violated the dignity of the unburied dead.

Nor, to be sure, was it reassuring to encounter other travelers who whether for reasons of injury, illness, or mental breakdown had ended up stuck or abandoned in the jungle. According to

Tamara, migrants arriving in Panama would often report stranded people, although it was generally impossible to establish their location given the lack of objective reference points or a proper map of the ever-fluctuating jungle route. On very rare occasions, the reports led to an uplifting outcome amid the brutality, as when a pregnant Haitian woman who seemed to have lost the will to live was extracted from the jungle following a collaborative effort involving MSF, local villagers, and a helicopter belonging to Panama's National Border Service (SENAFRONT). An Ecuadorean man had passed a mobile phone video along to MSF of the woman lying face down in a tent with her underwear around her ankles, largely unresponsive to attempts to rouse her. Against all odds, she was now recovering from the existential ordeal in Metetí, where she had availed herself of MSF's mental health services.

MSF had attended to tens of thousands of patients thus far, among them members of families that had been separated in the jungle—including children separated from their parents—as well as numerous victims of sexual violence. Particularly over the past month, Tamara said, there had been an increase in reports of migrants being forced to undress in the jungle and subjected to manual inspection for the purpose of uncovering any money hidden away in bodily orifices. The women were sometimes separated from the group for a more thorough revision—read: full-out rape—although men had also been victims of penetration. Some migrants reported sexual violence perpetrated by the people who had been paid to guide them through the jungle; others reported that these guides had delivered them directly into the hands of criminal bands who then went about robbing and raping. While MSF was equipped to administer post-exposure prophylaxis for sexually transmitted infections, the seventy-two-hour window of effectiveness meant that by the time most victims of sexual assault arrived to San Vicente or Lajas Blancas it was already too late.

In Spanish, incidentally, the verb *violar* means both "to violate," as in human rights, and "to rape"—and the Darién Gap is one of those places where the definitions compound one another in sinister amplification. In yet another testament to that fact in March of the following year, 2024, Panamanian authorities would order MSF to suspend its medical activities in the Darién after the organization was too annoyingly vocal about the spike in sexual violence in the Gap and Panamanian government inaction to curb the impunity. Over the span of 2023, a total of 676 people were treated by MSF for sexual assault in the Darién—a number that itself hardly reflects the magnitude of the problem given the frequent reluctance of victims to report such crimes in their precarious state as people on the move with notably scant human rights. In January 2024, the same month I would enter the Darién Gap from Colombia and decidedly the "low season" in terms of jungle crossings, 120 people were treated—nearly 18 percent of the total for the previous year. And in just one week in February, prior to receiving its shutdown order, MSF reported treating 113 people for sexual assault, including 9 children. Reports of mass sexual violence were also on the rise, including incidents involving more than 100 migrants at a time.

The Darién is not the only global migration hot spot where sexual violation attends the movement of vulnerable people—whose status as "migrants" often has more than a little to do with the reality that their rights have already been soundly violated in one way or another. Take Libya, a primary departure point for Europebound refugees fleeing war and economic misery, where, with the collusion of the European Union and particularly Italy—Libya's twentieth-century colonial masters and genocidaires—twenty-first-century migrant detention became a brisk business characterized by rape, slavery, and torture.

Then there is the sexual violence that has permeated Australia's offshore migrant-processing regime on the Pacific island nation of Nauru and Papua New Guinea's Manus Island, places that have also made headlines for their epidemic of migrant suicides and self-harm. Or consider September 2023 Reuters headlines like "Migrants Are Being Raped at Mexico Border as They Await

Entry to US"—the introduction to which article went as follows: "When Carolina's captors arrived at dawn to pull her out of the stash house in the Mexican border city of Reynosa in late May, she thought they were going to force her to call her family in Venezuela again to beg them to pay $2,000 ransom. . . . Instead, one of the men shoved her onto a broken-down bus parked outside and raped her." The dispatch quoted a U.S. Department of Homeland Security spokesperson as lamenting that "the inhumane way smugglers abuse, extort, and perpetrate violence against migrants for profit is criminal and morally reprehensible," a condemnation that conveniently excises from the equation the role of U.S. inhumanity—absent which, of course, migrant smugglers would be without a job.

But back to February 2023 in Metetí, where Tamara eventually decided I was not the worst journalist ever and even deviated from standard practice by allowing me an interview with MSF's mental health manager, Marilen Osinalde. Also Argentine, she had formerly been stationed in Liberia, Palestine, and Uganda and had spent her three months in Metetí thus far attending to migrants who had suffered sexual and other violence. To Marilen I posed the simple question: "What is the psychological explanation for the evil things that happen in the jungle?" The short answer was that "cruelty is human"—but there was a longer answer, too.

Culturally, Marilen explained, with Tamara chiming in from the sidelines, cruelty manifests itself in diverse ways; some people rape, some people bomb, some people erect border walls. The common denominator, by and large, is that the perpetrator of cruelty does not view the "Other" as a human being. In the case of rape, she said, the phenomenon is rather more complex than the Western stereotype of rapists as "psychopaths who grab you in the street in the night." In the Darién Gap and along other migration routes, for instance, the landscape of sexual aggression has to do with asserting power, status, and impunity, as well as with marking territory—speaking of borders. The use of rape as a "weapon" in the jungle—whether by Indigenous inhabitants, paramilitaries, or assorted criminal actors—objectifies and dehumanizes the migrant "Other," further solidifying power structures.

Noting that many of the sexual assailants are young men, Marilen speculated that in some cases the violence might amount to an initiation ritual of sorts. Rape is intended to "sow a certain terror," not so much to deter other migrants from coming as to show who is in charge and above the law—free to destroy individual dignity "and by extension the family." As Marilen talked I couldn't help but dwell on the fact that, while migration itself is criminalized, crimes against migrants are permitted to flourish with impunity as the cruelty of U.S. border policy plays out on migrant bodies. In the sadistic U.S.-fueled war on migrants, both rape and border walls are useful armaments.

Journalist Todd Miller's book *Empire of Borders: The Expansion of the US Border around the World* also came to mind, given that the Darién Gap seemed to be as good a U.S. border expansion as any. As Miller writes, we currently inhabit a world "whose battlefields are at the edges of where the rich and powerful meet the poor and marginalized, who must be managed, confined, and pacified" in the interest of perpetuating elite hegemony.[42] And what do you know: the U.S. border model has itself been "paramount to the scaffolding of the current order of the globe, managing the antagonisms . . . between the haves and have-nots."[43] Among these antagonisms is the obscene discrepancy in the right to engage in that most human action of movement, and Miller highlights the "enormous chasm between those who have freedom of movement and those who do not."[44]

In that sense, then, the Darién Gap is at the frontlines of this chasm—a battlefield on which the poor and marginalized from Peru to Burkina Faso to Bangladesh converge to confront the unseen forces of the global rich and powerful by penetrating the elite-imposed boundaries that are meant to confine them. Unlike the U.S.-Mexico border wall, the Gap is a naturally occurring barrier, and yet both landmarks serve the same fundamental purpose: they confer criminality upon U.S.-bound have-nots, while also functioning as physical and psychological weapons and formidable reminders of the violence that is par for the course for those denied the freedom to move. Granted, Donald Trump's reported vision of a U.S.-Mexico frontier entailing a "water-filled trench, stocked with snakes or alligators" and a wall with "spikes on top that could pierce human flesh" has yet to pan out, but it seems death by dehydration and heatstroke in the desert is probably scary and painful enough.

Recalling the Cuban women I had met in jail in Tapachula who had apparently suffered vicarious trauma after bearing witness to rape in the Darién Gap, I asked Marilen how one goes about treating traumatized people who, having just emerged from the jungle, are in emotional limbo with no opportunity for closure—and who are still potentially facing plenty more trauma on the road ahead. Acknowledging that the obstacles are substantial, Marilen stressed that it is key to offer as safe a space as possible under the circumstances in the migrant reception centers, remarking that many patients who have seen their dignity violated at every turn find it therapeutic simply to be treated with respect for a change. Rendering the psychological panorama all the more complex, of course, is that migrants are often fleeing traumatic situations in their home countries to start with, or are traveling under immense pressure to get to the United States—as in situations in which families have sold everything they own in order to fund the trip. Mothers traveling with children are frequently driven to extreme guilt and anguish by the scenes of death and violence being inflicted upon their kids, and a number of MSF's patients in Panama have turned up as repeat patients in Mexico.

When I later spoke to Guailis, the wife of the Venezuelan Jesús whose life had been saved by the dead person's hand, she told me that her two-year-old son Jhayden had mostly seen their ten-day jungle crossing as an adventure; she, however, had cried every night. Belisario had dropped me off at the roadside shack Guailis and Jesús had rented in Metetí after retrieving me from the Aruba, where I had been busy mystifying the Chinese patrons with my behavior. I had requested to purchase the blue sheets off of my bed, to which request they had acceded and remade the bed, replacing the now-purchased blue sheets with orange ones. I was then tempted to buy these, as well, but managed to channel the temptation into simply manically ordering sheets of various colors off the Internet, to be delivered to my rented house in Zipolite.

The bedsheet-buying frenzy had come about as the culmination of a period of a few hours in which I had convinced myself that I wanted to own a house—an urge I had not had since I was maybe nine years old—after seeing one advertised in the Zipolite Facebook group, with window shutters the same blue as my Aruba sheets. I had always avoided ownership and responsibility like the plague and could not for the life of me commit to living in one place or even remaining still in a single location for more than a few weeks or months. The coronavirus plague had put a temporary halt to my dashing about, but even after a year and a half straight in Mexico the suggestion that I actually "lived" there sent me into fits of anxiety. And yet here I was suddenly fancying myself a homeowner, with the only conceivable explanation being that it was some sort of obnoxious reaction to the phenomenon of migration and seeing a whole bunch of people on the move in situations of utter precarity. Fortunately, it was quickly established that I did not possess sufficient funds to acquire the blue-shuttered house—or any other, for that matter—and that anyway a yoga center was scheduled to open next door, which would have meant a constant stream of other white people and a continuous aneurysm. For the time being, then, it seemed acquiring way too many bedsheets was a good enough approximation of stability and control over the universe, and for good measure I also bought a hair brush from the Chinese-run store next to the Aruba, despite having literally not brushed my hair since 2003.

In her late twenties and with a scattering of tattoos, Guailis was from the Venezuelan state of Carabobo; her name was a combination of her parents' names, she explained with a shrug and smile. Belisario had descended from his taxi long enough to greet her, toss Jhayden in the air, and promise to return for me later. Inside the shack, Guailis apologized for the lack of chairs, and we arranged ourselves on a thin mattress on the floor, while Jhayden went about throwing a foam ball at me and pinching my nose. Clad in a T-shirt with a picture of a green velociraptor and the words "Caution: Raptor Trainer," Jhayden was then given the cell phone to watch a velociraptor cartoon with songs about velociraptors, which kept him distracted until the phone charge ran out.

In Venezuela Guailis had been studying to be a nurse, but as she had to pay for all of her training materials herself, it had eventually become prohibitively expensive, and she had given up. It was a far cry, no doubt, from the Venezuela I had visited in 2009—before the United States went maniacal on sanctions—when during a hitchhiking expedition through northern South America with my Polish friend Amelia we had checked ourselves into neighborhood health clinics purely for the novelty of receiving medical care that was entirely free of charge. Prior to fleeing the United States, my final run-ins with the American health care system had included an unfathomably priced cervical operation, mostly paid for by my parents' insurance, after which it had been impossible to undergo a gynecological checkup anywhere in the world from Mexico to Turkey without being asked in horror what third-world doctor had gotten a hold of my cervix. In Venezuela Amelia and I had also inserted ourselves into Hugo Chávez's February 2009 referendum campaign pitting *Sí* against *No*; we were on the side of the ultimately victorious *Sí*, and our campaign duties mainly consisted of dancing in Chávez shirts in the back of a truck.

When Guailis and Jesús left Venezuela for the United States, she told me, her six-year-old daughter stayed behind with Guailis's aunt, having announced that no way was she going in "that selva." Guailis, Jesús, Jhayden, and Guailis's four-month-old green-eyed pit bull Brandon boarded the bus to Medellín and then another bus to Necoclí, where due to high demand they had waited for eight days for a boat to Capurganá. In Capurgána they were subjected to a form of "psycho terror," as she put it, by the custodians of the Darién Gap, who warned them against trying to enter the jungle on their own unless they wanted to be killed. It was mandatory to hire a guide, the fee for which they were told was $150 per person; Guailis and Jesús did not have this amount, so green-eyed Brandon was taken as payment instead.

The family was put in a large group of other travelers, among them four children, all of whom were affixed with bracelets to indicate that they had been properly extorted in Capurganá—although the "continuous robbery" hardly ended there, Guailis said. Porters in orange vests offered to help carry bags, a service that then ended abruptly with a charge of twenty or thirty dollars issued to the bag's owner. As Guailis narrated her ten days in the jungle, there was an almost biblical creation story element to it, with most of the narrative segues consisting of: "And then it started to rain." Visual evidence of abundant rainfall was forthcoming in a cell phone photo she showed me of Jesús slathered in mud from the waist down, holding Jhayden pietà-style against a backdrop of an all-encompassing mud-scape.

The group's guide had rushed them through the first stretch of mud, insisting that it was imperative to arrive at the Panamanian border by four thirty in the afternoon. Upon arrival, the guide disappeared and a group of ten hooded men descended upon the group to relieve them of their valuables, which included most of Guailis and Jesus's remaining funds and one of their phones. The other phone, hidden in a diaper, had avoided confiscation. "And then it started to rain."

Guailis had not been raped, but she had heard about plenty of rapes, particularly on the route from Acandí, and had seen plenty of *muertos*, some of them rolled up in blankets. She had met a Haitian woman whose six-month-old baby had drowned when a piragua overturned; the pair had been en route to join the baby's father in the United States. Then there were all the stories of the Darién Gap's past victims that haunted Guailis on her journey, such as that of the six-year-old Venezuelan child shot in September 2022, about whom many a TikTok had been made. Indeed, perhaps social media was to thank for Guailis's own six-year-old's decision that under no circumstances was she setting foot in "that selva." Guailis spoke, too, of an Ecuadorean boy whose foot had split open and who was attended to by none other than a couple of Venezuelan doctors who were themselves migrating.

Every step of the way came with its own price, it seemed, with fees negotiable on an individual or group basis. At one point, Guailis said, the group negotiated passage of a certain stretch for sixty dollars and four telephones. To cross a river, individual payment was demanded based on nationality and socioeconomic profiling, and travelers from China and India were charged considerably more. At night the group camped by the river, and Guailis and the children cried—minus Jhayden, who apparently only cried when anyone tried to remove his velociraptor shirt or when the cell phone died, as I was able to witness during our time together. The phone was plugged in, the raptor cartoon resumed, and all was again well in the world.

Guailis and Jesús had entered the Darién Gap with three bags between them but had emerged with a small sack of medications and nothing else, having found it necessary to abandon the extra weight. They had seen crocodiles and monkeys, and after ten rain-filled days they had arrived at the Indigenous village of Canaan Membrillo, where they were then loaded onto piraguas to Puerto Limón before being bused to the migrant reception station at San Vicente. In Puerto Limón Guailis had met a Venezuelan man who was trying to figure out what to do with the one-year-old Ecuadorean baby girl that had been entrusted to him in the jungle by her mother; as Guailis told it, the baby had stopped eating and the desperate mom, who was unable to move at a rapid pace, had handed her off to the more agile Venezuelan in the hopes of getting her to a doctor as quickly as possible. Guailis didn't know if the mother had ever turned up in San Vicente, but she had observed that the baby didn't seem to want to let go of the Venezuelan man: "He was the only thing she knew for the past few days."

There followed the onset of Jhayden's diarrhea, the family's escape from San Vicente, and Jesús's procurement of employment at the Metetí car wash. One evening while Guailis was waiting for him to get off work, SENAFRONT officials had scooped her up and returned her to San Vicente, citing an impromptu made-up law according to which Venezuelans could not be on the street after 7 P.M. Somehow, she talked her way out of confinement, Jesús continued working, and the SENAFRONT folks eventually accepted them as interim residents of Metetí, she said, even waving to them at times. The day before I visited Guailis, Jesús had earned six dollars for an entire day's worth of labor, and she reckoned they would stay on for another two months or so before hitting the road again. When I asked whether the ten-day odyssey in the jungle had been worth it, she paused for a moment before responding: "I think so because we survived. You have to live it to tell it."

Guailis was hoping to avoid entering the United States illegally and had planned to apply for an appointment at the border via the CBP One app, which she had found out about thanks to TikTok and I had found out about thanks to her. At this point in my life I still had yet to grasp what an app even was, but further research revealed that U.S. Customs and Border Protection (CBP), an agency within the Homeland Security Department, had unveiled the "CBP One™ Mobile App to streamline lawful travel to United States," available in the Apple App Store and Google Play.[45] According to the CBP website, "all noncitizens without documents sufficient for lawful admission to the United States may register and request an appointment with the CBP One™ app" at an official "Port of Entry" to present their asylum claims—a process that was far easier said than done, as I would learn firsthand the following year when Johan would spend months battling said CBP One app.[46]

Beyond the fact that the system was conveniently constantly crashing, there were numerous other issues, as well—an obvious one being that many people on this earth are not technologically literate and especially not when dealing with programs that are deliberately fucked. Journalist John Washington has highlighted some additional glitches: "The technology seems unable to recognize many faces, especially when people have darker skin tones or Indigenous features—when they don't look like the blonde model on the screen's background. . . . Advocates are finding that Black asylum-seekers, from Haiti and African countries, or elsewhere, face greater bias using the app, as the algorithm doesn't recognize their skin tone."[47] If CBP One didn't pan out, Guailis told me, then it was up to God to get her and her family across the border.

Belisario rematerialized to transport me back to the Aruba, where I had little time to contemplate any further bedsheet purchases. No sooner had he departed than Belisario was again messaging me on WhatsApp to notify me that he had encountered a group of migrants with children walking on the side of the road—an uncommon sight given the Panamanian government's insistence on busing their undocumented guests to Costa Rica. Back he came to the Aruba and back we went to find the group, who were now resting in the semi-shade of a decrepit bus stop on the side of the Pan-American Highway just past the National Bank of Panama.

They were ten people in all, an extended family of farmworkers from somewhere in the vicinity of the Venezuelan city of Barquisimeto. There were three men, an obese woman in a white dress with red flowers and plastic sandals with socks, an older boy and two younger ones, two preteen girls, and a baby in a dirty diaper. Like Guailis and Jesús, they had crossed from Capurganá and had spent ten days in the jungle, with ubiquitous insect bites to show for it. One of the men remarked that, while he hadn't really believed beforehand what people said about all the *muertos* in the selva, he could now confirm it was absolutely true; there were bodies floating in the river, and he had seen a dead mother with two dead children and a man who had hanged himself nearby, whom he presumed to be the father.

Another of the men informed me that to get through the jungle, you had to "be like Spiderman" at times, while the husband of the obese woman volunteered that his wife was not pregnant, she was just fat, but she was used to farmwork and strong and had thus managed the "Spiderman" segments. At the migrant reception station at Lajas Blancas the family had all come down with diarrhea, and, lacking the forty dollars per person that the Panamanian government was charging migrants for the bus to the Costa Rican border, they had decided to set out on foot. The immigration authorities at the camp had initially urged them to think of someone abroad to call to send them funds for the bus fare via Western Union or any of the other unscrupulous money-transfer services that inevitably informally incarnate themselves in places with heavy migrant traffic—as I would soon see in Bajo Chiquito, where a cardboard sign advertised the local "Wester Union" branch. Naturally, these services entailed even greater highway robbery in migrant camps than they did in the outside world, with some "Wester Unions" reportedly absorbing 40 percent of transferred funds. At any rate, the Venezuelan family did not know anyone who could send them money, which, after all, was part of the reason they were migrating in the first place.

The next suggestion from the *migra* at Lajas Blancas, the family said, was to work in the camp until the bus fare had been paid off. They declined the offer of forced labor, and, rebuffing the warning from SENAFRONT officers that it was forbidden to leave the reception station on their own—and that they would surely be killed by criminals if they did so—set out walking to America, as it were. When I met them they were still more than 700 kilometers from Costa Rica, after which followed four more countries including the vast expanse of Mexico. Right here in front of me, then, were the "invading invaders" bleated about by the likes of Laura Loomer, ambling menacingly toward the U.S. border in flimsy plastic sandals from thousands of kilometers away. After seeking my advice on where in the United States they might direct themselves to look for farmwork, the family from Barquisimeto politely bid me *adiós* and continued the invasion.

Indeed, expanding on that old Cuban dictum about how no one leaves their country and walks through the selva for a week if they don't have to, it should also go without saying that no one walks from Venezuela to the United States without perceiving it to be distinctly necessary for survival. Those of us accustomed to freedom of movement would no doubt do well to spend more time contemplating the sheer physical agony of walking—not for the purpose of leisure or to reach a proximate destination but in an indefinitely prolonged state of extreme vulnerability and exposure to the elements. Nowhere, perhaps, is this agony more palpably displayed than on Mexico's Isthmus of Tehuantepec in the southern state of Oaxaca, just a few hours east of Zipolite—and still five countries away for the Venezuelans of Barquisimeto—where the privileged motorist may encounter the sight of an unending procession of migrants staggering along the side of the highway. Once one of the top contenders for the location of the world's first interoceanic canal, the isthmus is known for its spectacularly fierce winds, which have toppled many a cargo truck and constitute daunting obstacles to pedestrian movement. Add to the mix a punishing sun overhead, nothing but parched earth and windmills for as far as the eye can see, and the ever-present possibility of treacherous run-ins with organized crime and Mexican law enforcement outfits alike, and the landscape becomes almost surreally hostile. During one of my visits to the Isthmus of Tehuantepec in November 2023, I would be told by more than one migrant that they would take the Darién Gap over Mexico's "concrete jungle" any day.

Even in my own days of less elite forms of travel like hitchhiking, I never did much walking. Amelia and I had become unnaturally obsessed with hitchhiking in 2003 on the Greek island of Crete, where we met during a one-month certification course for teaching English as a foreign language, which had been the only future that had occurred to me after graduating from Columbia with a degree in political science. English-teaching aspirations were, however, quickly abandoned in favor of thumbing our way across countries and continents, a practice that enabled us to exist almost entirely for free for varying lengths of time in between bouts of employment at an avocado packing facility in a village in Andalucía, Spain, where we resided gratis in the house of a benevolent construction worker from Morocco named Abdul. When in 2004 Amelia and I spent three months in the southern Turkish coastal town of Fethiye, the hitchhiking got so out of hand that rather than trek a few hundred meters up a hill to the apartment where we were being hosted by a benevolent Turk, we would remain at the bottom with thumbs outstretched until someone indulged our slothfulness—itself often a result of overindulgence in Turkish rakı and cigarettes.

In retrospect, then, there had always been an inherent entitlement to my movements through the world, including ostensibly non-elite expeditionary undertakings, that kept me from having to walk when I didn't feel like it. Hitchhiking from Turkey to Syria in 2005, for example, Amelia and I were spared having to cover on foot the not insignificant distance between the Turkish border checkpoint at Cilvegözü and the Syrian one at Bab al-Hawa, as we were picked up by a Syrian man returning from a lengthy permanence in Serbia. The man's friend was waiting at Bab al-Hawa to welcome him, and the two of them then got to spend the better part of their day persuading the Syrian border guards to grant us entrance to the country, which they ultimately did, even though I had failed to procure in advance a Syrian visa as required. Amelia was traveling on her Polish passport and had the added advantage of not being from a country that had declared Syria part of the expanded "axis of evil."

In September of the following year, 2006, Amelia and I once again hitchhiked from Turkey to Syria, where I was once again admitted despite arriving without the proper paperwork. This time, we proceeded on to Lebanon, which had just been on the receiving end of a monthlong Israeli assault that had killed twelve hundred people and reduced sections of the country to rubble. The undertaking had transpired with the diligent assistance of the United States, which, never one to miss out on an Israeli slaughter-fest, had rush-shipped bombs to the Israeli military, while U.S. secretary of state Condoleezza Rice touted the carnage as the "birth pangs of a new Middle East" and president George W. Bush invented the adjective "Hezbollian."

In Lebanon, too, we barely had a chance to walk anywhere—which was probably fortuitous as Israel had just dropped some four million cluster bombs on the country, a large percentage of which had failed to explode. My own country's role in Lebanon's present decimation notwithstanding, Amelia and I were picked up, driven around, hosted in people's homes, overfed, plied with Lebanese wine and arak, and even gifted a giant Hezbollah wall clock to hitchhike back to Turkey with several months later. At 10,452 square kilometers, Lebanon is just about twice the size of the Darién Gap, and Lebanese driving habits ensure that the national mantra according to which it is only five minutes from the mountains to the sea is not in fact much of an exaggeration—when bridges and roads have not been blown up by Israel, that is. And yet the excessive hospitality extended to us came with its own implicit recognition of inherent privilege; the same treatment would not have been accorded to, for example, a pair of Beirut's Bangladeshi sanitation workers or Ethiopian housekeepers or Syrian laborers.

In Meteti I still had two locations at which to attempt unauthorized entry before heading back to Panama City and on to Mexico: Lajas Blancas, the reception station where migrants were transported after exiting the jungle at the Indigenous village of Bajo Chiquito, and Bajo Chiquito itself. Belisario signed on for both missions, and we drove to Lajas Blancas first, which required turning off of the Pan-American Highway and following a gravel road. Heeding Tamara's critiques of my wardrobe, I wore grey sweatpants, dirty sneakers, and a long-sleeved Palestine soccer shirt that covered my superabundance of bracelets. Unlike at the San Vicente reception station, where a lone SENAFRONT officer had been manning the entrance, Lajas Blancas offered a more chaotic milieu, with migrants milling around out front and lining up to board the Costa Rica bus. While Belisario busied himself fidgeting with his hands, I walked past an array of SENAFRONT and immigration officials and into the camp, which was reminiscent of the Siglo XXI jail in Tapachula insofar as there was laundry hanging from every possible surface from which it could be hung. Everywhere, people with dazed expressions reclined on the ground and in tents. Through the mud, a family pushed a wheelchair bearing a woman whose feet and legs were swollen and smothered in white cream. In addition to skin diseases contracted in the jungle, many migrants arrive in Panama with respiratory illnesses or mosquito-borne afflictions.

I had been in the camp no more than two minutes when a SENAFRONT guard appeared beside me and demanded my nationality. Having failed to prepare a suitable response to this question, I answered truthfully, and once we had established that I was not in fact migrating to my own homeland, I was deposited back at the entrance. Before leaving, Belisario and I chatted with a ten-year-old Venezuelan boy who had just arrived with his parents after six days in the jungle and who provided the requisite tally of *muertos*. His parents had run out of money, the boy said, so they might be staying in Lajas Blancas for a while. I thought about what I had been doing when I was ten, and it seemed to me that I had been riding horses and going to gymnastics class.

The excursion to Bajo Chiquito took place on February 26, 2023, the day before I was to depart for Panama City. In contrast to Lajas Blancas, the village fell inside the Darién Gap and could only be reached by car in the dry season—roughly December to April, not accounting for climate change fuckery—when a bridge was constructed over the Chucunaque River, only to be swept away again by the ensuing rains. A local Panamanian tour guide had offered to get me a piragua to Bajo Chiquito and the requisite SENAFRONT permission for $450, but Belisario had saved the day and had brought his Panamanian wife Elizabeth along, as well, who cited "tigers and snakes" as the reason she had never set foot in the jungle. So as to draw less attention, the taxi was left at home and the three of us instead crammed ourselves into the cab of Belisario's banged-up pickup truck; I had reprised the Palestine soccer shirt and grey sweatpants look, while Elizabeth sported a fake designer T-shirt and dangly gold earrings. From Meterí we drove southeast for well over an hour with not another vehicle in sight, crossing the provisional bridge over the Chucunaque as our sweat blended together and fused with the seat of the truck. Vegetation became denser and the road increasingly rough, giving the notes I attempted to jot down in my notebook the appearance of a seismic graph.

When we came upon the tiny Emberá village of Nuevo Vigia with its smattering of houses built on stilts, an Indigenous resident of the village stopped the truck and climbed into the back, announcing that he was also going to Bajo Chiquito. As we neared our destination we passed a group of people walking in the opposite direction; one man was limping to the point of requiring support by two others, and another man was wearing Venezuelan flag shorts. The vegetation gave way to a clearing, and Bajo Chiquito was upon us, spread out against the piragua-laden Tuquesa River. Our passenger directed us where to park the truck and kindly hooked me up with a bathroom belonging to an acquaintance of his in the village. I emerged to one of the more agonizing sounds to which I had ever born witness, which turned out to be coming from a giant pig that was being slaughtered by the river—and that very much did not want to die.

A sizable section of the village had been cordoned off to form a sort of open-air migrant holding pen, into which Belisario, Elizabeth, and I inserted ourselves unperceived by the Panamanian immigration officials consumed with registering piragua-loads of arrivals. In the span of just a few minutes, three piraguas pulled up to deliver several dozen more people, all of them wearing lifejackets—a charming touch, no doubt, for folks who had just survived a wide assortment of life-threatening perils in the jungle. Behind the congested registration area, a single individual was seated on the ground with outstretched feet clamped in wooden stocks, causing me to think the Panamanians had really taken migrant processing to a new level. However, Belisario informed me that the castigated person was a local, and that this was simply a method of punishment for petty thievery and other wrongdoings. An open umbrella had been placed over the stocks, which had thus far prevented the person from being barbecued by the sun.

In addition to "Wester Union," an array of other services had sprung up in Bajo Chiquito to cater to the guests in transit. A spot to put your tent would set you back between three and five dollars, while a shave cost three dollars, a telephone call cost one dollar, and a plate of chicken and rice cost five dollars. At one ramshackle eatery I heard a man tell his travel companion to decide whether they should have something to eat or something to drink, as there was not enough money to do both. Belisario, Elizabeth, and I made our way to the far side of the camp, stepping around tents and stray dogs. At a plastic water tank, a man filling a bottle received a shouted warning from a village resident that the water had yet to be purified; when he persisted in filling, the shouter shrugged: "Well, don't say that we killed you."

Over the past few years, Bajo Chiquito had undergone quite the dramatic shift on account of the astronomical spike in migration via the Darién Gap. A 2023 report on the village's transformation by Panamanian journalist Grisel Bethancourt, published jointly by Panama's *La Prensa* newspaper and the Latin American journalism platform Connectas, put Bajo Chiquito's base population at three hundred—with up to twelve hundred migrants now arriving on a daily basis. Contending that the general plight of these migrants had constituted a "golden opportunity" for the villagers, Bethancourt noted that "the migration flow has caused most of the local indigenous population to abandon their work in agriculture and fishing," while Bajo Chiquito's young women had "stopped goldsmithing and basketmaking to manage restaurants, internet service shops, and currency exchange offices." The sudden influx of migrant money had furthermore inspired many of Bajo

Chiquito's inhabitants to renovate or expand their homes, work that according to Bethancourt was now performed by laborers contracted from Panama City at a rate of $6,500 per home—whereas previously the male members of the community had "simply got together and built their houses using wood and straw that they gathered from the jungle itself."[48]

To be sure, the casual stereotyping of Indigenous persons is nothing new, and the deployment of the term "golden opportunity" suggests a heartless avarice on the part of the inhabitants of Bajo Chiquito—who, keen to milk migrants for all they are worth, are only too happy to throw tradition to the wind. And yet the village's transformation in the face of an imposed crisis would seem to in fact be an entirely logical consequence given the context of poverty, high unemployment, and persistent government neglect of Indigenous communities in Panama. There is no electricity network or sewage system in Bajo Chiquito; as of the time of my visit, cell phone communication with the outside world required trekking up a hill to get a signal. The village's diminutive health clinic, which I later popped into with Belisario and Elizabeth, was staffed by a single doctor and a jolly nurse who exclaimed, "Can you believe it's only the two of us for all these people!"—to which the doctor added with a roll of his eyes: "That's the Ministry of Health for you." The pair lamented the shortage of medicines at the clinic and told me that patients suffering from anything serious had to be taken to Meterí, a trip that most of the year had to be made by river.

In other words, there was not much evidence around of the "development" that had been promised Indigenous communities by successive Panamanian administrations. Stephanie Kane, whose research among the Emberá of the Darién in the 1980s served as the basis for her book *The Phantom Gringo Boat: Shamanic Discourse and Development in Panama*, observes that the Darién jungle and its Indigenous inhabitants were "key" to the "grand schemes for Panamanian development" in the decades of the 1970s and '80s, when the Emberá by and large abandoned the "tactics of retreat and dispersion" that had been their modus operandi "since the Conquest." For the first time "in written history," Kane writes, the Emberá moved into villages, having been "encouraged by promises of participatory democracy and a semiautonomous forest reserve, and finding themselves increasingly locked in by the boundaries of nation-states, ramifying transport routes, and multiplying multiethnic populations." Rural development and the Indigenous movement into villages had been a particular focus of Manuel Noriega's predecessor Omar Torrijos and had been "backed by funding and expertise from the U.S. government and the Organization of American States."[49]

The phantom gringo boat that features in the book's title, a reference to a shamanic story told to Kane, functions as an "allegory for development," as the author notes—and ultimately encapsulates the illusory lure of U.S.-backed schemes to "develop" the world into conditions more suitable to neoliberal capitalist "conquest," if you will. Fast-forward four decades from the 1980s to a March 2024 *Al Jazeera* dispatch from Bajo Chiquito, which highlighted rampant poverty among Panama's Emberá-Wounaan population as a reason kids in the village were dropping out of school to work as piragua captains in the new migrant industry. Titled "How Migration Transformed an Indigenous Town in Panama's Darien Gap," the article remarked: "Experts say communities like Bajo Chiquito are drifting away from traditional agricultural practices like growing plantain and rice, instead importing processed food to satisfy their needs." Which is pretty much capitalism in a nutshell.

Of course, capitalism specializes not only in severing the bonds between humans and the earth but also between humans themselves, in keeping with divide-and-conquer logic. In her 2021 book *Border and Rule: Global Migration, Capitalism, and the Rise of Racist Nationalism*, scholar Harsha Walia determines that "in addition to migration being a consequence of empire, capitalism, climate catastrophe, and oppressive hierarchies, contemporary migration is *itself* a mode of global governance, capital accumulation, and gendered racial class formation."[50] Walia enumerates the "shared logics of border formation—displacing, immobilizing, criminalizing, exploiting, and expelling migrants and refugees," all of which function to "divide the international working class and consolidate imperial, racial-capitalist, state, ruling-class, and far-right nationalist rule."[51] In effectively pitting impoverished migrants against impoverished Indigenous communities, then, the system appears to be doing a bang-up job in terms of dividing the global have-nots. Meanwhile, the phantom gringo boat sails on.

After Belisario, Elizabeth, and I had made the rounds of Bajo Chiquito, we reencountered our passenger from Nuevo Vigia, who, it turned out, was also involved in the business of transporting migrants by piragua to Lajas Blancas. Belisario had vaguely explained to him earlier that we were interested in talking to people in the camp, and he summoned us over to a palm tree–shaded area by the river that was littered with plastic bottles, aluminum cans, and discarded rubber boots and clothes. There he and a few colleagues were conferring with a group of nine young men from Colombia and Venezuela on the matter of the twenty-five dollar piragua fee—and specifically the fact that none of them had twenty-five dollars. One of them was Johan, who didn't speak to me during our encounter but was the first from the group to message me on WhatsApp a few days later.

Johan and his friends Andrés, Felipe, and El Mono had made the acquaintance of the other five in Bajo Chiquito. There was Julián, a seventeen-year-old from Cali, Colombia, who was traveling in the company of an Afro-Venezuelan man named Javier, referred to by everyone as *El Cucho*—Colombian slang for an old person—on account of his thirty-eight years. There was another Colombo-Venezuelan pair who would separate from the group in Costa Rica, leaving just the *Siete Magníficos*, as my dad would appoint them. And there was Kelvis, a Venezuelan in his twenties who had previously lived in Chile, was traveling solo, and did most of the talking. Kelvis, too, would become separated from the group in Mexico when the other six were removed from a bus by Mexican officials fulfilling their duty to make life hell for U.S.-bound migrants. Having fallen asleep beside an elderly Mexican woman, Kelvis passed undetected by the forces of law and order—although, as he would tell me much later, he was discovered soon enough and hauled off the bus, as well, whereupon he made a break for it and ran for the hills. He eventually found his way to La Bestia and, following a close call with a cartel and a near-drowning in the Rio Grande, crossed from the Mexican border city of Piedras Negras into Eagle Pass, Texas, where he was detained for a month and then provisionally released into the United States, his definitive fate to be decided at some future point.

When I finally tracked him down on Facebook in November 2023—more than eight months after the Mexican bus separation and two months after I had returned from Madrid with Johan—Kelvis was in Denver looking for work and showered me with virtual blessings from God for my life and health. He had known nothing of Johan and the others since March, having had no phone until he reached the United States and having never added them on social media. Johan had tried repeatedly to locate him, a search that was complicated by his ignorance of Kelvis's last name as well as his conviction that his first name was actually Kelvin. I myself was only able to find him when, waking up at four o'clock one morning in Zipolite with an extraordinary hangover, my brain cells collided in such a way as to remind me that, at one point early in the group's trajectory, Johan had messaged me with a photo of bus tickets they had purchased with money I had sent them. A vision flashed before me of names and surnames being printed on these tickets, and, sure enough, a scouring of my WhatsApp history produced just such a photo with just such information.

At Bajo Chiquito Kelvis and the others had acquired a pot in which they were endeavoring to boil river water over a pitiful fire. Elizabeth inquired as to what they had envisioned putting in this pot, which Kelvis laughingly qualified as a good question and replied that they had rounded up some rice and lentils. In between supervising the fire operation, Kelvis told us how armed men had attempted to rob him in the jungle but, verifying that he had nothing to rob, had sent him on his way; other migrants had obligingly pulled out all of their money for the taking because, as he put it, "fear is a weapon, too." The consensus among Kelvis and his newfound companions was that, although they lacked the funds for onward movement, they would not go back in the selva for a million dollars, which the man from Nuevo Vigia and his colleagues apparently took as their cue to leave.

As the young men told it, the stench of decomposing bodies in the jungle had been otherworldly—a persistent reminder of the proximity of death—and yet there had also been something spectacular about this "green hell," where in places the water had been crystalline and they had seen fish the length of their forearms. At the end of our encounter each of the young men shook hands with Belisario, Elizabeth, and me, and Belisario snapped a picture of the rest of us. "See you in Mexico" was my final exchange with the group, which turned out not to be a perfunctory promise, after all, as fewer than six weeks later I rendezvoused with the *Siete Magníficos* minus Kelvis in Ciudad Juárez. Speaking of "hell," the rendezvous took place just after forty would-be asylum seekers died in a fire at a migrant detention center in the city when the jail-keepers refused to open the cell doors.

As we lurched in the pickup truck along the dirt road back toward Metetí, Belisario pondered what would happen if he decided to walk to Colombia through the Darién Gap. "I would need a passport," he mused. "Otherwise I would be illegal in Colombia." Elizabeth declared that she would not like to walk through the jungle, and that was the end of that.

Early the next morning I took the bus from Metetí to Panama City, where I would catch a plane back to Mexico for a few weeks before jaunting off to El Salvador for the one-year anniversary of the state of emergency declared by Salvadoran president and self-proclaimed "coolest dictator in the world" Nayib Bukele, who had purported to solve the country's crime problem by simply throwing a significant portion of the population in jail, criminals or not.

On the six-hour ride to Panama City the passenger next to me kept himself entertained with a never-ending series of cockfight videos on his cell phone, while I huddled under various layers of sweaters—the bus's air-conditioning scheme having apparently been modeled on the U.S. example—and compulsively inspected the group photo Belisario had taken the previous day on my own phone.

Kelvis was at the far left of the group, wearing athletic pants and a Yankees baseball cap with no shirt and flashing the peace sign. Andrés was next to him, shoeless in a Chicago Bulls jersey and giving the thumbs up, as were Julián and Felipe. I was at the far right sporting my red Mexican supermarket bag and the same Palestine soccer shirt I would wear into the Darién Gap almost a year later, and Johan was next to me grinning with one hand over his crotch, as would prove to be his go-to pose for photographs. Javier stared intently at the camera while clutching the piece of paper upon which my WhatsApp number had been scrawled; El Mono was absent from the photo, having been tending to the pot of river water.

Zooming in on the individual faces of the young men, I was simultaneously thoroughly invigorated by the defiant resilience they exuded and horrified at my utter triteness; inspiring as these kids may have been to the gringa passerby, who was I to exploit their circumstances for my own fleeting sentimental gratification? After all, there is nothing glamorous or romantic about being thousands of kilometers and a whole bunch of international borders away from your intended destination, without the proper paperwork or a penny to your name to get you there.

In the end, however, there was nothing fleeting about our interaction, and for the next two months the fate of the seven Colombo-Venezuelans would supersede in urgency everything else in my life—including work, sleep, and whatever modicum of mental stability I might have ever aspired to obtain—as I became all-consumed with getting them from Panama to the U.S. border. On the surface, my contributions primarily consisted of having a total nervous collapse as my friends were robbed and extorted, slept on roadsides and in bus terminals, and were scooped up by the *migra* in various countries after walking all day and returned to the border where they had started from. In addition to continuously losing my shit, I did serve a practical purpose, which was to collect money on PayPal from my Québécois friend Émile and other willing donors and send it, along with my own money, to the boys by Western Union via third parties conscripted for said transaction, as I myself had been inexplicably banned from Western Union. The whole process was further complicated by the fact that none of the seven possessed a passport or accepted document with which to withdraw transferred funds, meaning that at each new Western Union location they had to contract a local to receive the money on their behalf, and my notebook turned into a mess of names and nationalities. There was Vinicio Fuentes Fuentes of Costa Rica, Juan Alberto Noj Aguilar of Guatemala, and Belén Celeste Velásquez Moreno, who had escaped national identification by my pen. Meanwhile among the scores of WhatsApp messages exchanged on a daily basis with Johan, Felipe, and Julián—the ones who consistently had phones until Julián's was stolen—were numerous appeals to me to please calm down as stress was bad for my health. As I had made no effort to hide my feelings about the United States, they also amusedly followed my lead in referring to my homeland as the *país de mierda*, or shit country, and patiently responded to my intermittent anticapitalist tantrums with "Tienes toda la razón"—"You're so right."

Throughout all of this time, of course, I maintained my frenetic international movement, flitting from Panama to Mexico to El Salvador to Mexico to Suriname and so on, such being the prerogative of those of us to whom borders scarcely apply. But all the while, there was something incomparably moving about watching people reclaim their own right to move.

As my father lay dying of prostate cancer in August 2023 at the age of seventy-two, he emerged from the state of muteness that had seemingly permanently taken hold of him to recite vehemently the 1927 poem "Sailing to Byzantium" by William Butler Yeats, which begins: "That is no country for old men." The impromptu performance took place in my father's bed in the apartment my parents had rented just two months earlier in Washington, D.C., my own birthplace, and was attended by my mother, my uncle, and me. Following his poetic outburst, my dad resumed his silence, which was thereafter punctuated only by intermittent implorations that we kill him.

My parents had moved from Barcelona back to the United States in 2021, thus complicating my pledge to never set foot in the country again, and had settled briefly in Louisville, where my younger brother had taken up a post with the Kentucky Air National Guard after many years of service abroad with the U.S. Special Operations forces. This at least meant he was no longer participating directly in mass slaughter in Afghanistan and the Middle East; it was still Kentucky, however, which post-Barcelona did not quite cut it for my parents in terms of available cultural activities. So back they went to D.C., where in the 1980s my dad had cut his teeth as a reporter for The Bureau of National Affairs, Inc., subsequently acquired by Bloomberg. In 1989, when I was seven years old, we had moved to Austin, Texas, where I got to participate in rodeos and undergo indoctrination in a sequence of

Catholic schools at which my parents had determined my attendance would be prudent despite not being particularly religious themselves.

Upon repatriation my parents had found that the United States was indeed "no country for old men"—not that it was much of a place for anyone else, either. After being diagnosed with prostate cancer in late 2022, my dad's demise had been notably accelerated by the lucrative chemotherapy treatments pushed on him by his doctors against my mother's counsel, which had done nothing to deter the cancer and everything to ensure that his remaining time on earth was spent in pure agony. Then there was the medication prescribed to him, including a prostate cancer drug called Xtandi, which had been developed with U.S. taxpayer money but not, obviously, for the benefit of the average American cancer patient. Had they not applied for and received foundational financial support, my parents would have been billed no less than $14,579.01 for a one-month supply of Xtandi—that is, more than I myself had known to earn in an entire year. Of the many deadly faces of capitalism, the U.S. health care system is certainly one of them.

I had flown to D.C. from southern Turkey when it had become abruptly clear that my dad would not be around for nearly as long as had been expected. During my final week on the Turkish coast I had sought to spend as much time underwater as possible, and I expanded my swimming regimen—a holdover from my days as a competitive swimmer in Texas—in accordance with the American mantra that you must always be doing something productive even when your dad is dying. The butterfly stroke proved the least compatible with sobbing, and the whole routine was presumably even less advisable given that I had taken to consuming a bottle of wine for breakfast. When I was not submerged in the sea, I frantically made lists of the things I had to do, such as swim and eat—obsessive list-making being an apparent genetic inheritance from none other than my dad, whose addiction to grocery lists was no doubt material for some sort of psychological study or another. As the reality of a fatherless future set in, my lists became all the more manic, and I made lists everywhere and then lists of all the lists I had made.

My dad was a man of many, many words, which meant I could rarely get one in edgewise and which is likely what condemned me to the writing path. In possession of a collection of such curious habits as continuously reading *Don Quixote* from front to back in both English and Spanish, he was prone to stream-of-consciousness rambling that nonetheless garnered him enraptured listeners wherever he went, from the grocery store to the wine store to the park to the Barcelona community gym where he did as much chattering as exercising.

The silence to which my dad had been reduced in his final days thus constituted a sort of death sentence in itself. But when I first arrived in D.C. from Turkey, he was still able to speak, enough to impress upon me the importance of making haste to the ophthalmologist if at any point in my life I experienced the warning signs of a detached retina, which he himself had suffered in Barcelona. Although he could barely hold a pen, he undertook a painstaking artistic rendering of what your field of view looks like when you have a detached retina; handing me the piece of paper with a look of distress, it seemed that, while the retinal alert had been satisfactorily issued, there was still a backlog of preoccupations preventing him from dying in peace. Indeed, it had long been clear that, along with list-making, my own propensity toward neurotic fretting over dangers real and imagined was a genetic hand-me-down from my father, who in addition to his various real-life afflictions had also, for example, briefly come down with knee cancer after eating canned beans in 1971. I never was able to ascertain what had prompted this auto-diagnosis or how the beans had factored in, but starting in elementary school I, too, had suffered from a series of hallucinated ailments including epilepsy. For his part, my dad's dad—the D-Day-Korea-Vietnam veteran and SOUTHCOM military intelligence director—had regularly referenced an "altar of worries" that required constant tending. Many of these worries were also creative, as when the Russians were attacking his Texas nursing home and his fellow residents had started utilizing their oxygen tanks for communist purposes.

Prior to the onset of muteness, my dad had managed one final list, which I transcribed sitting on the bed next to him. It was a list of passengers for a 2024 boat trip off the coast of Turkey, the very coast from which I had just arrived and where my dad had determined his ashes should be scattered—specifically around the rope swing over the water where he had once impressed himself immensely by executing a cannonball into the sea at sixty-plus years of age. He had first visited me in Fethiye in 2007 during a pause in my travels with Amelia, our hitchhiking exploits being something my father boasted to his friends about while simultaneously accusing me of trying to incite heart failure in him. In Fethiye he accumulated various Turkish vocabulary words that he would forevermore delight in deploying: *dur* (stop), *git* (go), *iyi bayramlar* (the greeting for the Eid holiday), and *kanalizasyon*—which he learned by inspecting the sewage drains in the street. Incapable of sitting still unless it was to read *Don Quixote*, my dad would disappear for hours to return with a detailed report on the conditions of the local cemetery and the number of persons with the surname Kurt—his own middle name—contained therein.

My mother was herself a three-time breast cancer survivor and almost scarily superhuman, having shown herself without doubt to be exceptionally better than my dad and me at dealing with life. However, having to carry her companion of more than half a century to the bathroom while he disintegrated before her eyes had taken an obvious toll, leaving me to be the one who had to keep it together for the first time ever. This I managed by simply switching between wine and my dad's bourbon from the crack of dawn until night and thereby suspending reality, to be dealt with at a later point in time. On one of my excursions to the kitchen to refill my glass I came across a letter on my mother's desk, in my dad's handwriting and dated September 21, 1988. It was addressed to my brother and me—three and six years old at the time—and as per my mother's recollection had been penned during one of his phases when he convinced himself for no reason that he was dying. In the event that he wasn't around to watch us grow up, my dad wrote, he wanted to leave us with a bit of advice: "Wake up happy every morning, don't waste your lives worrying or making lists, and remember that I love you most."

In Barcelona I had regularly descended upon my parents' apartment, one of several international locations—along with Beirut, Sarajevo, and a friend's village in the southern Italian region of Puglia—that had been indefinitely burdened with suitcases full of my crap. To keep track of what crap was where, I made taxonomic lists populated by such items as "sequined leggings from Uzbekistan," "10-kilo book of Persian poems from dude in Isfahan," and "Ethiopian bowl-thing"—a cursory effort, perhaps, to prove that my existence was less of a scattered mess than it seemed. Although my aversion to making my bed and washing my hair was no doubt agonizing for a father whose commitment to orderly cleanliness drove him to polish the doorknobs and banisters in the apartment building lobby, he became increasingly weepy at my every departure and would accompany me on the bus to the Barcelona airport, worry beads in tow. In December 2019, we made what would turn out to be the last of these trips when I departed Barcelona for San Salvador three months before the outbreak of the coronavirus pandemic. At the airport security checkpoint my dad delivered a rather heart-wrenching little speech about how the papa bear didn't want anything bad to happen to the baby bear, an homage to one of my childhood bedtime stories.

And it was partly for this reason that I would not enter the Darién Gap beyond Bajo Chiquito while my dad was still alive, as I figured I had already done enough harm to his nervous system by spending twenty-four hours in a migrant jail in Mexico. He was aware, of course, that I was plotting something jungle-related, but he developed an immediate adoration for the *Siete Magníficos* and celebrated their every advancement in the direction of the United States despite his own distaste for a place that was "no country for old men." He would be particularly enthralled by a video Felipe made in Ciudad Júarez, after the *Siete* minus Kelvis had arrived on La Bestia and before I met up with them. Set to a song by an Argentine artist that began "Nadie dijo que iba a ser fácil / Nadie dijo que no hay que luchar"—"Nobody said it was going to be easy / Nobody said you don't have to fight"—the video commenced with Felipe, Johan, El Mono, and Andrés adjusting themselves in the mirror in a bathroom in Colombia. There followed footage of them traipsing through the jungle with machetes, them traipsing down the side of a highway with a large group of migrants, them looking highly displeased in the back of a Costa Rican law enforcement vehicle, and finally with Julián and Javier atop La Bestia, bundled up in all of the sweaters given to them by a friend of mine outside Oaxaca City. I also forwarded my dad a short video made by Johan of his newly gelled hair at the extortionately priced Airbnb I had procured for the *Siete* for one night in Tegucigalpa, where the exuberant Honduran proprietor gifted them some used clothes, as well. My dad pronounced Johan "cute" and used the Caracas connection to launch into a tale about his maternal uncle's sketchy involvement in U.S. oil machinations in Venezuela in the 1950s.

In reviewing my WhatsApp correspondence with my parents, I see that I sent them a slew of sniveling audio messages on April 8, 2023, the day my friends crossed from Juárez into El Paso in the company of a Cuban they had met, who had already been in the United States once and who claimed to know the ropes on the border. I had met up with the group the previous day, which we had spent making a beer-fueled spectacle in various bars down the street from the official border crossing, one of them cleverly called Coyote. Felipe had fallen while executing a move on the dance floor, and Andrés, who perceived Mexican musical selections as a personal affront, had undertaken to impose his own Colombo-Venezuelan playlist on the DJ. Seventeen-year-old Julián, with whom I was partnered for a salsa, concluded mid-experience that "Americans dance weird." Johan stayed with me for the night in a room I had rented, while the others slept outside in a plaza downtown so as not to offend the evangelicals who ran the shelter where they had been staying for a modest weekly fee. The evangelicals were offended all the same when the boys turned up early the next morning; having been declared personae non gratae at the shelter, it was decided that today was as good a day as any to cross into "los United"—but not before more beer.

I do not recall with great clarity the moment of our Juárez farewell, although I do recall subsequently stumbling around crying and then asking a policeman who the fuck he thought he was when he reprimanded me for drinking on the street. Mercifully, he chose not to escalate the situation, so I purchased yet more beer from a convenience store and sat slumped on a curb across from the railroad tracks upon which La Bestia itself was stopped, one of its yellow railcars bearing the Union Pacific insignia and the slogan "Building America." In response to my blubbering WhatsApp audios about how the *Magníficos* were going to be kidnapped or jailed or deported, my father—despite having his own issues to deal with at the moment, such as dying—texted back: "So sad and sorry belen. this reminds me of when you learned that there wasn't a santa . . . try to get some rest. and per mom's example always try to look on the bright side."

The possibility of a bright side emerged later that night when I received an ecstatic call from Felipe, who was in El Paso with Julián, El Mono, and Andrés. The four had been separated from Johan and the others during the border traversal and had ended up in the parking lot of a restaurant called Twin Peaks, a photo of which Felipe sent me when he couldn't pronounce the name and which appeared to be a suitably gaudy introduction to America. I frantically set about ordering an Uber to shuttle them to a shelter they had been told about, whereupon Felipe's phone died and communications duties were handed off to Julián. Collective cross-border nail-biting ensued as the Uber inched toward Twin Peaks, but just as the driver was turning into the lot and victory seemed imminent, who should turn up as well but the *migra*. There was shouting on Julián's end and a string of curse words in Spanish; then the line went dead, and I was left to deal with the driver, who scolded me for calling an Uber on behalf of illegals and warned me never to do it again.

Felipe would be the first to be released from *migra* detention and—having received a stack of unintelligible papers and a formal order to get the hell out of Texas—was soon on a plane bound for Boston, his airfare sponsored by Émile. He landed construction work almost immediately, and with his first day's payment sent his mother in Colombia a hundred dollars, spent the rest at the mall, and made a TikTok of himself strolling down the street swinging shopping bags. The others, however, would take much longer to achieve the American dream. Julián was carted off to a facility for juveniles in Tampa, only to be released months later to a relative in California. The three Venezuelans in the group—Johan, Andrés, and Javier—were detained for six days in Texas and then flown to Arizona, where they were redeposited over the border in Mexico. After some encounters with cartel folks in Sonora had prompted Johan to inform me that he could no longer furnish me with his daily promise that he would be OK, Émile procured the three of them tickets for a multiday bus odyssey back to Mexico City, where I booked them a room and ordered them arepas for delivery. Johan would then begin his homeward migration in preparation for Madrid, while Andrés and Javier opted to reboard La Bestia north, this time making it across the border and being allowed to stay for the time being.

El Mono, also Colombian, was released shortly after Felipe but had nowhere to go—until my father, his deteriorating state of health notwithstanding, pulled strings to land him a landscaping job with a Mexican American dude in Kentucky, one of many local residents my dad had charmed with his ramblings. Before passage was secured—once again courtesy of Émile—on the Greyhound bus from Texas to "Qitoqui," as El Mono would henceforth insist on spelling it, he got to experience the charms of El Paso for a number of long days and nights. On more than one occasion he called me crying to ask why it had occurred to him to abandon his two young children and a country where at least he was free for a place where life was impossible if you didn't have money and every-one—as far as he could tell—was too scared to help him. On top of it all he fell ill, and I received a selfie of him lying prostrate on an El Paso sidewalk sporting a baseball cap with an American flag, his eyes puffy and his nose red. The United States, in sum, was not a country for men young or old.

My father died on August 16, 2023, once my mother and uncle—my dad's brother, a doctor—had over-administered him morphine in accordance with his wishes to cease to exist as quickly as possible. He left behind various unfinished memoirs for posthumous editing by my mom, thanks to which manuscripts I would encounter new biographical details about my dad that had not made it into forty-one years of continuous monologues. I learned, for example, that my father had lost his virginity to a prostitute at the age of fifteen in Panama City, which had not been his idea but rather that of an older Canal Zone bully at Balboa High School and which had been a source of shame throughout his life. And I acquired more Fernández family trivia, one of my dad's very favorite subjects of study that encompassed both his maternal and paternal sides, as his mother had also been surnamed Fernández. His mother's father, José Fernández, had worked at a cigar factory in Tampa when, one fine day in the early 1900s, he had stabbed a fellow laborer for insulting the family and had been shipped off to Cuba by his sisters until the coast had cleared—whereupon he returned to Tampa and found work with Mafia boss Santo Traffi-cante. My dad's father, paternal grandfather, and paternal great-grandfather were all also named José Fernández, while my father was the first Joseph. As per one of the memoirs, great-grandfather José had been on the verge of taking his vows as a priest in the parish of Santa María de Ordoeste in Galicia, Spain, when grand-father José had come along, birthed by none other than Josefa, the cleaning lady for the priest's quarters attached to the church.

I also augmented my knowledge of my dad's dealings in Pan-ama Red in the late 1960s, which sustained him economically for a period in the United States following his return from Panama and which he acquired at a cost of three dollars per kilo, mailed to him from the Canal Zone in saltine cracker tins. During a brief stay in Seattle he was assisted in his operations by a couple of U.S. soldiers AWOL from the Vietnam War, and at one point the income was so substantial that my dad had to open a savings account. He shared his weed with Curtiss Harris, the defense minister for the Seattle chapter of the Black Panthers, who lived one floor above him and about whom my dad penned the following anecdote:

> In the short two-plus months we were there, Harris was shot in the knuckles while he stood on the front porch of our building. One of the young [Black Panther] recruits who was probably only 17 or 18 was shot and killed directly below our view window by a Seattle cop. What happened was that Harris and the kid were tinting the windows of a V.W. in the street down the hill from the apartment building . . . when a police patrol car stopped to "investigate." The kid ran and was chased up the hill toward our building by one of the policemen. When the kid wouldn't stop as instructed the cop shot him in the back.

Some things never change in the land of the free.

Once my father had been loaded into a bag for cremation and the bourbon supply, at least, had been exhausted, I stayed on with my mother in D.C. for a few weeks on autopilot as we came to grips with referring to my dad in the past tense. We sat for hours on the apartment balcony staring at the National Cathedral across the street, and my mother availed herself of the local medical cannabis program to keep her bong loaded. It was during the latter half of August that Johan's Venezuelan passport miraculously materialized, and he and I would then spend the month of September in Madrid not getting him settled. We did, however, settle on a plan for the Darién Gap in January, while also watching countless hours of the Pablo Escobar series in bed and having plenty of dramatic public quarrels on such important matters as whether Coca-Cola was bad for you. Plus, I got to reacquaint myself with the hormonal joys of the morning-after pill—but it would all be worth it in the end when Johan had my name tattooed onto his arm, where I would live happily ever after in the company of his mother and daughter. Then back Johan went to Venezuela and back I went to D.C. for another interlude with my mom before hitting up "home" in Zipolite for two months and returning to the United States for Christmas, the final step in my buildup to the jungle.

Home proved ever less capable of confining me, and no sooner had I arrived back in Zipolite than I was off to Tapachula, Chiapas, my former carceral stomping grounds that was itself known among migrants as Mexico's preeminent *ciudad-cárcel*, or "jail city." This on account of its function as a trap even for those international refuge seekers who were not physically jailed in the Siglo XXI detention center, but whose onward movement was nonetheless stymied by eternal bureaucracy and general fuckery by the Mexican state acting on behalf of the gringos. While the official rules governing migrant movement—and official interpretations of those rules—were in constant flux, in theory asylum seekers in Tapachula were supposed to solicit protection from the Mexican Commission for Refugee Assistance (COMAR). Only after receiving COMAR certification as bona fide refugees, a process that could take an eternity, were folks then ostensibly entitled to abandon the jail city and freely transit Mexican territory. And yet there were countless cases of refugees returned to Chiapas from other Mexican states after having their COMAR papers torn up by some official or another.

My plan in Tapachula was to shamelessly exploit the captive migrant population for interrogation purposes—and specifically to determine just how scared shitless I needed to be about entering the jungle. This was my second trip back to the city after my stint behind bars, the first having taken place in January 2023, the month before I met Johan and the others in Bajo Chiquito. Although the first trip had not been conducted solely with an eye to hounding people about the jungle, I had fallen into conversation with several survivors of the Darién Gap, including a young man from rural Haiti whom I met in downtown Tapachula's Miguel Hidalgo Central Park, just across from the golden statue of Benito Juárez, nineteenth-century icon and the first Mexican President of Indigenous origins. The wall behind the statue features Juárez's famed quote: "Entre los individuos como entre las naciones el respeto al derecho ajeno es la paz," meaning "among individuals as among nations, respect for the rights of others is peace." Not that the scene playing out in Miguel Hidalgo Central Park was at all suggestive of, well, "respect for the rights of others," consisting as it generally did of refuge seekers in varying stages of exhaustion withering under the sun, some of them clutching folders containing paperwork confirming that their refugee status applications had been submitted and were swirling around somewhere in the great void known as COMAR.

My Haitian interlocutor had been in Tapachula for two months and eleven days—but who was counting?—and was awaiting permission from the void in order to continue his northward trek, which had commenced in Chile and taken him through Bolivia, Peru, and Colombia, where he had entered the jungle from Capurganá. The crossing to Panama had taken him five days; he had seen many dead bodies and had been robbed of $200 by an assailant. In Tapachula I also met two Bangladeshi men, who intercepted me on the street to ask for help in locating the *paquetería*, as the translation app on their cell phone informed me. The *paquetería* in question turned out to be FedEx, and as we went in search of the office they explained in modified English that they had left Bangladesh for political reasons and had spent five months traveling via Africa to Colombia with their family, including two children. The Darién Gap had been a prolonged nightmare and had been preceded by some sort of maritime calamity in which many migrants had drowned. Out of funds and stuck in the jail city, the family had joined Tapachula's ever-expanding population of refuge seekers in torturous limbo.

For the hell of it I also hit up Siglo XXI, where the guards at the entrance said that, no, they did not remember me, and that, no, they did not feel like going inside to see if anyone else did. I had forgotten to bring along a copy of the book I had written about my jail experience, so that particular prime selfie opportunity was thwarted, and I took a seat on the curb outside the facility next to a young Honduran man named Diego, who was waiting for a friend. Diego had arrived three days earlier from Tegucigalpa, where he had lost his job at a bakery during the pandemic and had grown tired of living in a place where fear had "become normalized," as he put it. Although Honduras was only two countries away, the trip had been anything but simple; extorted by police all the way across Guatemala, he had come to the conclusion that humans treated one another very poorly. Crossing the river into Mexico in the early morning when it was still dark, he had taken a series of minibuses to Tapachula, descending from the vehicle before each immigration checkpoint to execute a loop around the installation on foot and boarding another bus on the other side. As COMAR conveniently maintained no presence on the actual Mexico-Guatemala border, this minibus routine had decreased Diego's chances of being detained and interned in Siglo XXI himself. He was now in possession of his very own COMAR paper guaranteeing him a response to his request for refugee status by October—that is, nine months later, whereupon he would continue on toward the United States so that any children he might eventually have would not have to grow up in normalized fear, too. In the meantime, he had found a job at a carwash earning approximately five dollars for eleven hours of work per day.

In Tapachula I additionally paid a visit to the municipal cemetery, a sprawling expanse overflowing with graves in colorful disrepair—including the remains of the previous November's Day of the Dead celebration—and an assortment of dogs who had sought to compensate for the oppressive heat by splaying themselves across the larger tombstones. Indeed, Mexicans may take the global cake in terms of celebrating the dead, as is perhaps best encapsulated by a report in Spain's *El País* newspaper, published two and a half months into the coronavirus pandemic, which dealt with Mexican graveyard closures and related social-distancing measures and bore the headline "La muerte ya no es una fiesta"—"Death Isn't a Party Anymore." Three men reclining on dilapidated benches near the municipal cemetery's entrance looked at me blankly when I asked to be directed to "the migrant section," before one of them corrected my terminology: "You mean the *fosa común*"—the mass grave. This was reserved for migrants who had perished undocumented and unidentified in Tapachula, with no family to claim them and leaving no trace that they had ever existed at all. In that sense it was not unlike the Darién Gap itself, a mass migrant grave in its own right.

I would find the mass grave in the very farthest corner of the cemetery, the men told me, gesturing in the direction I needed to walk and resuming their repose. So off I went through the jumble of colors and crumbling graves, intermittently stumbling upon tombstones inscribed with Chinese names—the legacy of an earlier era of migration—and in the very farthest corner I found dirt, grass, rubbish, and some scattered wooden crosses. Just to confirm that the abrupt aesthetic switch indicated that I was now in fact upon the mass grave, I approached two workers refurbishing a blue-colored tomb nearby. The older of the two men, Ramón, gave me his personal assurance that the patch of dirt I had seen was without doubt the *fosa común*, and he was certain of it because he had assisted in interring the initial set of seventeen anonymous bodies that had been delivered in bags.

This had been several years ago, Ramón said, but more unidentified remains were added later, and he now had no idea how many deceased migrants were riding out eternity in the far back corner of a Mexican graveyard unbeknownst to their loved ones, wherever they might be. Ramón had worked at the Tapachula municipal cemetery for thirty-five years and in response to my distinctly unoriginal question stated that, no, he had never felt scared because "it's the living you have to fear, not the dead." He even slept at the cemetery at times—as, it turned out, many a migrant had also done back in the day when the Tapachula railway station had served as the starting point of La Bestia. The graveyard's proximity to the station had made it one option for overnight accommodations for northbound migrants, who perhaps also detected less to fear among the dead than the living. In 2005, railroad damage wrought by Hurricane Stan pushed La Bestia's starting point to the city of Arriaga, Chiapas, northwest of Tapachula; nowadays, migrants must travel more than 1,000 kilometers from Tapachula to the municipality of Huehuetoca north of Mexico City for a chance at boarding La Bestia.

My second post-carceral return to Tapachula took place in early November 2023 just after the Day of the Dead, which I had spent at the hilltop municipal cemetery of Zipolite jumping out of my skin at every war zone–worthy explosion of fireworks. As per tradition the graveyard was awash in the *cempazúchitl* flower, or Mexican marigold, along with food, drink, and cumbias blasting from various sound speakers. The name Zipolite is said to mean *playa de la muerte*, or beach of death, in a local Indigenous language— there being some disagreement as to which one—and the cemetery population included victims of Zipolite's savage sea as well as folks killed for narco-related reasons.

As I was incompetent in nearly all things requiring physical skill, a Mexican companion of mine had also done me the favor of erecting an elaborate Day of the Dead altar on the patio of my rented house, with countless *cempazúchitl* tied with great patience onto a palm frond arch. On the altar were offerings of fruit, nuts, hot chocolate, beer, mezcal, and fresh tamales, which were an immediate hit with the ants. Using clothespins I had acquired the previous year in Havana, Cuba, I affixed to the arch a large photo of my dad in scarf and cap as well as a printed image of the Palestinian flag, which seemed only appropriate in light of the genocide that had recently been launched by the Israeli military in the Gaza Strip. My own country's complicity in the undertaking would remain steadfast, and half a year into the slaughter the U.S.

Congress would approve $26 billion in supplemental wartime aid to Israel—not to be confused with the billions of dollars the United States already flings at the country on an annual basis. Granted, Biden made a few noises about withholding certain weaponry from the Israelis because "civilians have been killed in Gaza as a consequence of those bombs."[52] But this, after all, is the whole point of genocide, and, needless to say, business continued as usual. The Gaza Strip was converted into a mass grave, thousands of children were buried under the rubble, utter depravity was normalized, and Ramón's observation about the living versus the dead rang increasingly true.

For my second return to Tapachula my dad was no longer around to freak out about the prospect of having to once again deal with "The ASSHOLEs" at the U.S. embassy in Mexico City, who had hung up on my mother when I was in jail and who were consistently capitalized in my dad's WhatsApp missives. In his honor, I once again booked myself a room at the Hotel Cervantino a few blocks from Miguel Hidalgo Central Park, which in its lobby boasted a statue of Don Quixote, protagonist of my dad's most-read book. I would later learn from Todd Balf's book *The Darkest Jungle* that there was a Quixote connection to the Darién Gap, too, and that lieutenant Isaac Strain—head of the catastrophic U.S. Darién Exploring Expedition in 1854 that had explored the wonders of starving in the wilderness while being consumed by botflies—had taken to reciting passages from Cervantes's work for morale-boosting purposes.

I was welcomed at the Cervantino by the same Salvadoran receptionist—we'll call her Dulcinea—whom I had met during my last stay at the hotel, when an early-morning excursion to the hallway coffeemaker wearing one of my many El Salvador soccer jerseys had turned into an hour-long conversation. It was thus that, circa 5 a.m., I had learned the reason for Dulcinea's own migration to Mexico twelve years earlier, which was that her daughter's elementary school bus had been hijacked by MS-13 one afternoon and driven up into the Salvadoran hills for three hours of terror. The students were ultimately left unharmed, but the bus driver was killed in front of them, Dulcinea said, as a warning to the other bus drivers to keep on top of their extortion payments to the gang. Her daughter had been returned to her with bloodied clothes, as the children had thrown themselves on their beloved driver's body urging him to wake up. Twelve years had passed, Dulcinea told me with a shake of her head and a guilty half-smile, and she still wouldn't let her daughter go to the corner store by herself.

It bears underscoring that, while it has been the preferred narrative of successive administrations in both the United States and El Salvador to portray MS-13 and the other Salvadoran gangs as singularly and organically monstrous, they are in reality nothing but a direct result of U.S. policy. The chain of events is straightforward: Once upon a Salvadoran civil war of 1979–92, which killed upwards of seventy-five thousand people, the United States fervently backed the right-wing military that was responsible—along with friendly paramilitary groups and death squads—for the vast majority of the "serious acts of violence," according to the U.N. Truth Commission on El Salvador. On account of this violence an untold number of Salvadorans fled north to the United States itself, many of them to Los Angeles and environs, where things weren't exactly peaceable, either, and gangs formed as a means of communal self-defense. Following the war's end, the United States had the bright idea to deport Salvadoran gang members en masse to a devastated nation, where the ensuing U.S.-backed neoliberal assault left many Salvadorans with no options for maintaining a livelihood or social support network aside from gang membership. And voilà: a gang menace was born—a perennial bogeyman that would, in the ostensible absence of all-out war, forevermore justify draconian domestic militarization schemes and the right-wing obliteration of human rights.

Dulcinea and the other Cervantino receptionists would play an eager role in my November 2023 migrant interrogation operations and would rush to alert me whenever there was a new hotel arrival who had traversed the Darién Gap. Obviously, this was a cohort of migrants with access to funds to pay for hotel accommodations and not representative of Tapachula's overall population of refuge seekers—not that the Cervantino was ranked high up on the list of luxury hotel offerings in Chiapas. When I was released from Siglo XXI in July 2021, for example, two immigration officials had deposited me at the One Tapachula hotel, which—even with the *migra* discount to which my captors had so magnanimously entitled me—was still nearly three times the price of the Cervantino. As neither Dulcinea nor any of the other receptionists spoke anything but Spanish, they relied on a cell phone translation app that was beyond my technological grasp but that enabled them to communicate with guests from Afghanistan to China. Dulcinea had been gifted an ornate bracelet by a family of Afghan refugees who had departed prior to my arrival, but thanks to her colleague's intervention I had been able to speak in the hotel lobby with four young Afghan men who had flown to Brazil and from there worked their way up to Necoclí, Colombia. There they had caught the boat to Capurganá and then another boat to Carreto in Panama—a shorter and pricier route than those taken by most navigators of the Darién Gap, which had taken them one and a half days and put them back $750 each. They had been guided by gunmen, the four men told me in English, and there were "so many people walking you will think you are in a hallway." Our chat having concluded, I endeavored to make supplementary small talk by asking how Afghanistan was these days, to which the reply was raised eyebrows all around and the rhetorical query: "I guess you watch the news?"

The Cervantino reception staff were bummed when by a few minutes I missed an Uzbek family in traditional dress who had been turned away from the hotel due to lack of rooms, but an excited knock at my door one afternoon produced the news that some Ecuadoreans were in the lobby. I was in the middle of being violently ill on account of a Salvadoran pupusa restaurant I had been prematurely thrilled to stumble upon in downtown

Tapachula, but as Ecuadoreans were one nationality I had yet to accost in the Darién Gap context, I pried myself away from the toilet and followed the receptionist out.

The Ecuadoreans consisted of two women, one man, and two young children, a girl and a boy. They hailed from the Andean highlands and, if things went as planned, were bound for Minnesota. They had crossed from Acandí and had spent three and a half days in the jungle, where their encounters with *muertos* had included a freshly drowned corpse; they had also witnessed an entire family nearly be swept away by the river current. In some places the water level was so high that it reached the adults' necks, and crossing the river required forming a human chain with other migrants. When I asked the kids if they had been scared, the little girl responded with a defiant shake of the head, while the little boy's mother answered on his behalf: "Este sí." They had not been robbed in the jungle, but the folks behind them had, and they had run out of food midway through the trip. Furthermore, they did not recommend *la ONU* in Panama for anyone wishing to preserve their dignity. Plan Minnesota had come about as a result of the lack of employment opportunities at home and an ongoing wave of unchecked lethal violence.

My original plan to utilize Miguel Hidalgo Central Park as an additional one-stop shop for migrant interrogation had been derailed by Tapachula's powers that be, who had fenced off the entire area for renovation, which conveniently prevented migrants from continuing to congregate there. Of course, there were still the surrounding streets as well as the whole rest of downtown Tapachula, where it was not exactly difficult to track down the city's multitude of international guests. But things were not helped when I suffered one of my periodic bouts of thoroughly incapacitating shyness, in which I convinced myself that I wasn't even worthy of talking to anyone anyway—clearly not the most effective mindset for conducting journalism. When in these moods my sole consolation was a few lines from the late American journalist Joan Didion, whose self-definition as "neurotically inarticulate" I also heavily sympathized with: "I am bad at interviewing people. . . . I do not like to make telephone calls, and would not like to count the mornings I have sat on some Best Western motel bed somewhere and tried to force myself to put through the call to the assistant district attorney."[53]

I didn't need to make any phone calls, obviously, but I did need to try to channel my dad's passion for speaking to strangers, as I had imposed on myself the requirement that I needed to interact in Tapachula with at least one Venezuelan and at least one Haitian—these two nationalities being among the most consistently represented in the Darién Gap. I decided to get the Haitians out of the way first and set out on foot from the Cervantino to make my rounds of the Tapachula city center, all the while racking my brain for a less-than-super-annoying way to strike up conversation. I resolved to approach Haitians on the street to inquire where downtown I might find Haitian food, and to go from there.

The first several people I intercepted spoke only Haitian Creole, and since I had yet to master the phone translation app—not that I ever would—the interaction ended there. Then came a girl who spoke sufficient Spanish to direct me to a small eatery just off the central park that served only Haitian fare. I arrived at the place to find that the food was not yet there, as it was being prepared in another location, but out front was a Haitian woman in a blue off-the-shoulder top and yellow spandex shorts who had lived in Chile for seven years and with whom communication in Spanish was thus smooth. In her thirties and presiding over a bucket filled with bottled water, Coca-Cola, and energy drinks for sale, Natacha promised me that Haitian food was well worth the wait.

Natacha had made the journey from Chile with her two-year-old and her husband, whose job it was to babysit while she sold cold beverages on the street, a business that entailed running from the police multiple times a day with her bucket and then returning to sell again. Her clientele was strictly Haitian, she told me, as the *blancos* bought their beverages elsewhere. She had been in Tapachula for several months already awaiting a response from COMAR to be able to proceed north to the U.S. border and had two additional children in Haiti whom she had not seen since leaving for Chile; one of them, in fact, was turning twelve years old this very day. Upon learning that I myself had not reproduced at all, Natacha assured me that I was not too old and there was still time.

When I told Natacha that I would be entering the Darién Gap in January and was more or less scared out of my mind, she laughed and said not to worry. She and her family had crossed from Acandí, and the trip had taken them a few days. Yes, they had seen *muertos*, and yes, it had all been horrible and difficult, and yes, it was psychologically excruciating to find oneself helpless and at the mercy of the elements in the middle of a vast nothingness—but not to fear, I would be fine! Vats of food then started rolling up and Natacha shooed me into the eatery, where I joined two Haitian men, both of them sporting "Bryant 24" Los Angeles Lakers jerseys, as the first customers. The Haitian fellow in charge of ladling served me a dollop from each vat, which proved so filling that half of the plate ended up going to a Guatemalan migrant who had popped in to see if there were any leftovers.

It should be noted that nowhere has the profoundly fucked nature of racialized U.S. anti-immigration policy been so egregiously apparent as in Haiti, where, immediately following the January 2010 earthquake that killed more than two hundred thousand people, the U.S. Air Force dispatched a plane to fly for five hours per day broadcasting a public service announcement in Creole from Haitian ambassador to the United States Raymond Joseph: "Listen, don't rush on boats to leave the country . . . because, I'll be honest with you: If you think you will reach the U.S. and all the doors will be wide open to you, that's not at all the case. And they will intercept you right on the water and send you back home where you came from."[54]

And yet it wasn't just the crass response to nearly a quarter of a million people being crushed to death that rendered the whole airborne spectacle so ludicrously sinister. Despite consistently closing its doors to Haitian refugees, the United States has a solid history of busting down Haiti's doors whenever it pleases—entitlement to shameless and unrepentant hypocrisy being one of the perks of imperial status. There was that time in 1914 that U.S. marines raided Haiti's central bank in the capital Port-au-Prince and made off to a Wall Street vault with "half the nation's gold reserves," as former Associated Press correspondent in Port-au-Prince Jonathan M. Katz wrote in a July 2021 *Foreign Policy* article titled "U.S. Intervention in Haiti Would Be a Disaster—Again." The article, which illustrates how Haiti's "poverty and chaos has been shaped by Washington for decades," goes on to detail how the marine heist helped pave the way for an "all-out invasion" by the United States, which during its ensuing occupation of the country for nearly two decades "reimposed forced, unpaid labor, performed at gunpoint, to build a road system to ensure military and commercial control."

Again, the perennial moral of the story is that the only border that ever matters is the U.S. one. Although Ambassador Joseph's 2010 aerial message specified that "they will intercept you right on the water and send you back home," the American government had also floated the possibility of diverting intercepted Haitians to the U.S. naval base at Guantánamo Bay, which had by then already made a name for itself as an offshore penal colony and torture center on occupied Cuban land. This would not have been the only time, however, that Guantánamo was utilized as a holding pen for Haitian refugees, who had the dubious honor of being the facility's very first guests in the 1990s, when thousands were indefinitely detained as they fled Haiti in the aftermath of the 1991 U.S.-backed military coup against president Jean-Bertrand Aristide—not to be confused with the 2004 U.S.-backed coup against Jean-Bertrand Aristide. Other U.S. activities in Haiti included supporting dictators François "Papa Doc" Duvalier and Jean-Claude "Baby Doc" Duvalier as they went about killing tens of thousands of Haitians, an arrangement that understandably also caused many people to flee the country. And in 2011, WikiLeaks cables revealed that the Obama administration had worked to block an increase in the minimum wage for Haitian assembly-zone workers, whose labor on behalf of U.S. clothing manufacturers was deemed worthy of thirty-one U.S. cents per hour and not a penny more.

Washington's outsized hand in shaping "poverty and chaos" in Haiti notwithstanding, a helping American hand was not extended to those who, like Natacha and her family, had to deal with the fallout, since that would defeat the whole point of imperialism. Whether by sea or via the Darién Gap, Haitians continue to risk their lives to journey to the country largely responsible for making their own country unlivable—a country where the doors are only "wide open" in right-wing Republican fantasies of Democratic plots to flood the United States with migrants. As I paid my lunch bill in Tapachula at the door of the Haitian eatery, Natacha dashed by with her bucket and a smile, the police in languid pursuit.

To complete my Tapachula checklist I still needed to track down at least one citizen of Venezuela, another nationality well acquainted with U.S. efforts to complicate existence. U.S. sanctions on Venezuela were initially imposed by George W. Bush in 2005 during the reign of Hugo Chávez and were intensified by Donald Trump in January 2019 with the goal of assisting Juan Guaidó—the little-known right-wing character who had just taken the liberty of auto-proclaiming himself interim president of Venezuela—in achieving his dream. Never mind that there was already a president of Venezuela by the name of Nicolás Maduro; the United States went ahead and recognized Guaidó anyway, and the Trump administration appointed a special envoy to "help the Venezuelan people fully restore democracy and prosperity to their country."[55] This was none other than Cold War criminal Elliott Abrams, whose claims to fame included having been convicted for his role in the Iran-Contra affair, arguing that Guatemala's genocidal dictator Efraín Ríos Montt had "brought considerable progress" in the field of human rights and helping to incite the failed 2002 coup d'état against Chávez.

The "restoration of democracy" ultimately failed and Guaidó ended up in Miami, which was as good a place as any for a self-declared interim president of Venezuela. In the meantime, sanctions worked their magic, with U.S. officials making no bones about the fact that the Venezuelan public itself was the intended target of economic warfare; in March 2019, secretary of state Mike Pompeo delivered an eloquent progress report to the press: "The circle is tightening. The humanitarian crisis in increasing by the hour. . . . You can see the increasing pain and suffering that the Venezuelan people are suffering from."[56]

Like with Cuba, the U.S. blockade of Venezuela aims to prove that socialism doesn't work—when in reality all it proves is that socialism doesn't work so well when it is under prolonged savage attack by capitalist superpowers intent on annihilating any positive alternate example. Nor, to be sure, does U.S. propaganda always work even on those who abandon Venezuela for *el sueño americano* (the American dream); Johan and his friends, for example, all idolized Chávez.

The "suffering that the Venezuelan people are suffering from" was still visible four years after Pompeo's assessment in an infographic on the "deadly impact of sanctions" on Venezuela, published in March 2023 by the Venezuelanalysis website using statistics from the Center for Economic and Policy Research, the U.S. Government Accountability Office, the U.N. Food and Agriculture Organization, and other sources. In addition to being responsible for outbreaks of previously controlled diseases and rendering some 2.5 million people food insecure, coercive economic measures had caused more than one hundred thousand deaths as of 2020. As of 2019, Venezuelanalysis calculated, 22 percent of children under five were stunted on account of sanctions, which had also resulted in deteriorated domestic infrastructure and shortages of water, electricity, and cooking gas.

In August 2023, the U.N. Refugee Agency reported that "more than 7.7 million people have left Venezuela in search of protection and a better life"—which is why I found it confounding that I could not for the life of me locate a Venezuelan to talk to in downtown Tapachula, now that I had made it my mission.[57]

Several attempts to engage in ethnic profiling failed, and a family I could have sworn was from Venezuela turned out to be Honduran. Consisting of a mother, four children, and a visibly ill infant, the family had fled the fantastic levels of violence in Honduras only to be robbed of everything they had in Guatemala. There was another reason aside from the desire for personal safety that they needed to reach the United States, the mother told me, which was that her eldest son was buried in Kansas City, Missouri, where he had died in 2022 at the age of thirteen, apparently by drowning. If she could not cry at her son's grave, life simply could not go on, and thus the family would somehow have to make it to Missouri with the zero resources they had at their disposal. As she spoke with me, the children ran in circles, stopping to inspect my bracelets, and the baby in her arms sucked on the barrel of a small plastic gun.

Further ethnic profiling led me to a barbershop not far from the Haitian eatery, where I concluded that the handful of young tattooed dudes being groomed to reggaetón music blasting from a speaker must surely be Venezuelan, the establishment being an almost exact replica of a Venezuelan-run barbershop Johan had patronized in Madrid. The dudes were not Venezuelan, they themselves informed me, and hailed instead from Cuba, but suggested a certain street corner where the chances of finding Venezuelans were high and I would no doubt hear plenty of stories about the selva and the *muertos*. One young man from Havana sitting on the barbershop stoop related a secondhand story he had heard from some Venezuelans about a man whose infant was swept away by the river current: "It happened right in front of their eyes. They had to watch it." A Colombian then popped in to ask why the Venezuelans were being looked for and offered his own Colombian-ness as close enough. It was quickly revealed, however, that he had not crossed the Darién Gap and like the Cubans had managed to fly to Nicaragua—at which point the Cuban from Havana remarked: "OK I realize the selva is hard, but try being deported from Mexico to Cuba and having to come up with four thousand dollars again when you don't even have enough money to eat." In other words, perhaps, it's not just the jungle that's a jungle out there.

On a whim I boarded a minibus from the city center out to COMAR's base of operations at the Tapachula Ecological Park, located near a neighborhood someone had seen fit to name *Pobres Unidos* (United Poor People). As these minibuses were not particularly known for caring whether passengers survived the ride, I sat up front with the driver to better brace myself against screeching halts and minimize the possibility of being flung into someone's lap. I had other things to worry about, too, such as that the torrid afternoon heat had resulted in a pool of sweat accumulating beneath my ass, which I futilely tried to mop up with my shorts as I descended from the vehicle and for which I had no time to even apologize as the minibus careened off.

COMAR had already closed up shop for the day, but a gaggle of police was lolling about, and, in the wide traffic median just beyond the COMAR station was, lo and behold, an extended family of ten from Guanarito in the Venezuelan state of Portuguesa. They had arrived in Tapachula the previous day and erected a tarp in the median, where they were now cooking rice in a large pot someone had gifted them after all of their cooking equipment had been confiscated by Panamanian authorities when they exited the jungle—"They thought it was weapons," one of the male children explained with a mix of sarcasm and amusement. As the family had swiftly ascertained that waiting in the median for months while COMAR considered their case was not a viable option, they would begin walking to Mexico City in the morning, "with the grace of God."

Opting to not beat around the bush, I told the family that I would be entering the Darién Gap in January and was rather petrified—might they have any counsel? This set off a full hour in which all ten family members alternately advised, warned, reminisced, philosophized, laughed, cried, and cooked rice. As had happened with the *Siete Magníficos*, I caught not a single name during this first encounter with the family and would only go about filling in such biographical gaps as we remained in contact over the coming weeks. The most vocal members of the group were two sisters, both in their thirties, named, as I would eventually learn, Isamar and Yurbis; the former was petite to the point of earning the nickname *La Chiquita*, while the latter was sturdy and buxom. The other eight members of the family included two of Isamar and Yurbis's brothers, two of Isamar's kids, Yurbis's husband and two kids, and a cousin. One of the brothers had been in the Venezuelan National Guard, meaning that he would be in deep shit if deported to Venezuela. Prior to embarking on the odyssey to the United States, Isamar's family had resided for a spell in the Colombian department of Nariño near the border with Ecuador, where she had worked as a hairstylist and her younger son had "worked as a student," he told me with a grin. Yurbis's family had lived in the impoverished Bogotá suburb of Soacha—a place associated, inter alia, with the "false positives" scandal that rocked the U.S.-backed administration of Álvaro Uribe but didn't stop Uribe from being memorialized in *The Wall Street Journal* as "The Man Who Saved Colombia." After all, rewarding Colombian soldiers for executing civilians and passing the corpses off as left-wing guerrillas is tantamount to "saving Colombia," right? The scandal broke in 2008 when the bodies of teenagers and young men from Soacha turned up in the department of Norte de Santander abutting the Venezuelan border—the same Colombian department where Johan would later work on a coca plantation.

The family had entered the Darién Gap via Acandí, and the crossing had taken them three days. It had rained the whole time. The official price of passage was $280 per person, which had taken a while to be negotiated down to a quantity that was within the realm of possibility. Their funds having been thus exhausted, the bright side was that "they couldn't rob us in the selva because we didn't have anything to rob." I myself should not take any cash with me into the jungle, they advised, and it would be a plus if I knew how to swim. I was to follow the blue plastic bags marking the good path, not the red plastic bags marking the bad one. I should wear slip-resistant shoes, and by no means should I be deceived into wearing boots. I should take plenty of water and food; Isamar's son suggested instant soup. If possible, I should also try to look more like a man, and I should try to speak like a Venezuelan. There commenced a review of signature Venezuelan terms, with which I had of course been thoroughly familiarized during my month in Madrid with Johan along with more obscene Venezuelan lingo. The family then reverted to the consensus that perhaps it was better if I just didn't speak—although I would have to speak at least a little, they said, so as not to arouse suspicion.

I gave them the rundown on Johan and explained that he and his brother would be accompanying me into the selva, in response to which Yurbis noted that "sometimes men are weaker than women" and encouraged me to ensure beforehand that the two men in question would die along with me if I had to die. Despite the subject matter, this advice was not imparted forebodingly but rather with a spirit of camaraderie and a dimpled smile—and the family reckoned that, since Johan and his brother were Venezuelan anyway, they could just do all the talking for me. Yurbis's husband Darío, who was alternately tending to the pot of rice and tending to the needs of a thirsty kitten who had shown up, stressed upon me the importance of never trusting "people walking in the opposite direction in the selva because they are *personas muertas*," which I assumed was some sort of metaphorical pronouncement before I realized he meant it quite literally. They had passed one old man, he told me, who was heading back in the direction of Acandí, and had asked him if it was still a long way to go until Panama; he had instructed them to keep going straight and they'd get there, but when they turned around a second later the old man had vanished into thin air.

As for the cadavers in the jungle, the family could not tell me how many they saw in total, but Yurbis affirmed that "I can say that we have all stepped on dead people." The stench of bodies in advanced stages of decomposition was difficult to expunge from one's nostrils and seemed to cling to the clothes and skin, as well. On one occasion, a hand protruding from a tent had belonged to a dead pregnant woman; a different time, a woman's hair extending from beneath a tree branch indicated yet another unburied corpse. "You need to be psychologically prepared for the selva," Isamar declared, "because sometimes it is like a horror movie in there." If I wasn't in a good spot mentally, she said, it would be unwise to attempt the trip, as preexisting stress and anxiety would just be exacerbated by the sun and a ton of other factors and I would end up "trapped in despair." I made a mental note to sort out all of my neuroses by January.

Sitting cross-legged on the ground in calf-length black sweatpants and a ragged blue T-shirt full of holes, Isamar was at present the only one in the group with a functioning phone, and it was she that I would remain in regular contact with on WhatsApp as they navigated Mexico over the coming weeks. In addition to keeping me apprised of every misdeed by the Mexican *migra*—who at one point forcibly separated the family, sending them to different locations in Chiapas only to regroup with great difficulty and a lot of extra walking and sleepless nights—Isamar sent me photos of her "*princesa*," her eighteen-year-old daughter Francis, from whom she had never been apart and who was clearly the center of her world. Francis had been left behind in the care of her grandmother as Isamar could not bear the thought of anything happening to her on the journey, but the plan was to work as hard as she could in America to send Francis money to open a small business of some sort. As with the other members of the family, the ultimate goal was not to remain in the United States but rather to return to Venezuela with enough money to live. From the photos of Isamar and Francis in tight jeans, crop tops, and matching dyed red hair, I gathered that the sweatpants and ragged T-shirt look had required some adjusting to.

According to Isamar, "paranormal things" happened in the jungle, and at night you heard "wailing from the mountains." Dishing out rice from the pot, Yurbis agreed that "there is something in that jungle that puts you in a bad place"; at the same time, though, there was great natural beauty to be admired amid the horror. Darío reminisced about the "crystalline water," while Isamar's son warned me that "you have to cross a river for like two days," which caused everyone to laugh. Of the whole group, the only two who said they would consider setting foot in the jungle again were Darío—who told me that, if his schedule weren't fully booked at the moment, he would have been happy to escort me—and José, the non-ex-National Guard brother of Isamar and Yurbis. Isamar's son advised me against accepting José's offer, as he ate far too much and we'd be loaded down with food.

Another prerequisite for entering the selva was hardening your heart, the family told me, because if you tried to help everyone who needed help you'd never get out yourself. They had apparently failed at following their own advice and had assisted a Haitian man who had been abandoned by his family as well as a Haitian woman with a two-year-old child. The woman's pants had ripped between her thighs, and she had developed a severe chafing rash. The family could keep talking to me forever about the jungle, they said, but in the end I would have to "see, hear, and feel it" for myself. At some point my face must have assumed an expression of utter terror as they switched into pep talk mode: "We know you can do it!"

Some final advice was imparted—don't drink the river water, watch out for slippery rocks, ask God to guide you—and I gave the family the bulk of the Mexican pesos I had on me. It was only fair compensation, to be sure, for their having taken the time to provide a ten-person crash course in Darién Gap survival despite their own precarious existential predicament and the fact that they would literally be sleeping in the middle of the road. We took the obligatory group photo in the traffic median and made the obligatory promise to meet up in the United States, and the children told me they were sure I wouldn't die in the selva. Death was also mercifully avoided on the minibus back to the city center, where for two dollars I acquired a glittery unicorn wallet, acquisition of glittery unicorn paraphernalia evidently being the latest manifestation of post-midlife crisis.

Little did I know I would see the family again just over two weeks later, on November 23, in the village of Santo Domingo Ingenio on Oaxaca's Isthmus of Tehuantepec, home of the notoriously fierce winds that have been the demise of a many a Mexican cargo truck. I had come by bus from Zipolite to spend a few nights in the isthmian city of Juchitán, which had become a prominent migrant crossroads and therefore a prominent node for migrant extortion; near the bus terminal, some enterprising person had even tacked a neon green posterboard advertising CBP One appointments onto a tree. Wandering into the López Lena Palace hotel in downtown Juchitán, I found it jam-packed with citizens of Mauritania and a smattering of Saudis. A friendly fellow from the Mexican state of Sinaloa who was involved in extortion operations openly told me that the migrants were being bused from Juchitán to Mexico City for "about ten thousand pesos" per person—almost $600. In the hotel lobby, pictures of Frida Kahlo adorned the walls, and two women seated at a table handled passports, stacks of one hundred dollar bills, and a credit card machine. The Sinaloan and his colleagues laughed at my query as to whether the buses would be stopped by the *migra*.

At the López Lena Palace I spoke with a thirty-five-year-old Mauritanian man named Moussa, who was clad in an Old Navy U.S. flag T-shirt. To navigate the language barrier I called my former Lebanese-Palestinian boyfriend in Beirut on WhatsApp to communicate with Moussa in Arabic, although the combination of Mexican and Lebanese Internet service constituted a formidable barrier in its own right. Moussa had not crossed the Darién Gap, having flown from Turkey to Colombia and then proceeded to Nicaragua. He was an active member of a Mauritanian anti-slavery movement persecuted by the government and feared for his arrest and torture if deported. Once again, then, I had found myself face-to-face with one of Laura Loomer's "invading invaders"—this time in the immediate U.S. backyard.

As luck would have it, Isamar then messaged me to report that the family had arrived in nearby Santo Domingo Ingenio with the latest migrant caravan to have departed Tapachula, which they had joined along the way in the hopes that it might confer safety in numbers. These caravans, too, provided much fearmongering fodder in the United States; when the first such caravan had set out from Honduras in 2018, Trump had broadcast a "National Emergy [*sic*]" on Twitter, citing "criminals and unknown Middle Easterners . . . mixed in" with the pedestrians.[58] I negotiated taxi fare with an older cab driver out to the village, which lay some forty-five minutes northeast of Juchitán via the wind-ravaged highway. It was incidentally Thanksgiving, and while I did not usually keep track of holidays celebrating the genocide of Native Americans, perhaps something in my gringo subconscious compelled me to buy a heap of fried chicken to take to the family.

As the taxi lurched in the wind past migrants traipsing along the side of the highway toward Juchitán, some of them carrying babies or pushing strollers, the driver declared that he wished he could just snap his fingers and "resolve all of this suffering." He couldn't even give migrants a hand by offering them a ride, he lamented, as he'd quickly get busted by "the cartels." He deposited me close to Santo Domingo Ingenio's central pavilion, where the caravan was meant to sleep for the night and which was ringed by balaclava-sporting contingents of Mexico's National Guard. Isamar and a few of the kids hobbled over to greet me and escort me back to the plastic sheet that was serving as the family's bed, and Isamar cried over the fried chicken, crate of bottled water, and extra pesos I had brought. She cried again over the paracetamol I purchased at the local pharmacy for José, who was shivering and wrapped up in a blanket on the floor. Yurbis laughingly showed me the sanitary napkins she had inserted into her pink plastic clogs to temporarily resolve the issue of the gaping holes in the soles and asked if it was obvious that the collective mood had deteriorated since our meeting in Tapachula. Shoes and feet had been torn up by continuous contact with scorching pavement, and the family had been on the receiving end of various objects thrown at them by local inhabitants, with Mexican hospitality presumably not aided by certain fantastic rumors that had seemingly taken root as fact. Case in point: a resident of Tapachula—the wife of a Mexican marine, no less—had recently sworn to me that president López Obrador was paying migrants $500 a month.

All in all, the family had concluded that, the horrors of the Darién Gap notwithstanding, they would take the selva over Mexico's "cement jungle" any day. That same night back in Juchitán, I received word from Isamar that the caravan had been dislodged from Santo Domingo Ingenio and moved to a village in the opposite direction of that in which they needed to go—meaning that their trek would now be that much longer as they were forced to retrace their steps in disintegrating footwear. Two days later, I had returned to Zipolite, but they were still in the same isthmian village, where it had come to their attention that caravan participants were being kidnapped and held for ransom. Exhausted and scared to death, they separated from what remained of the caravan to face being blown over by the winds of the Isthmus of Tehuantepec on their own. Arriving in Juchitán on foot, Isamar contacted me for a geographical consultation concerning the proper route; as I had just traveled from Juchitán to Zipolite by bus and knew there were no immigration checkpoints between Juchitán and the next major city, Salina Cruz, it occurred to me to suggest, for the hell of it, that they try hitchhiking that far to give their legs a rest. And so it was that the family from Guanarito in the Venezuelan state of Portuguesa beat hands-down every hitchhiking achievement I had to my name, finagling a ride for ten people as far as Salina Cruz and then another ride almost all the way to Mexico City in the back of an open-air truck, whose driver had apparently decided he could care less about immigration checkpoints.

The plan in Mexico City had been to apply for the CBP One appointments at the U.S. border, as the family figured they'd had enough of crossing rivers. When the CBP One app proved indecipherable and they had nothing to live on, however, they concluded that their only option was to board La Bestia—the very train from which a former Venezuelan neighbor of theirs had recently fallen and died. Nearly a week was spent on the rails, stopping and starting and changing trains, while I remained characteristically calm throughout, stalking Isamar's daughter Francis on Facebook for any sign of news after Isamar's phone died and then harassing Francis directly. They finally turned up in the Mexican border city of Piedras Negras and attempted to cross into Eagle Pass, Texas, with a large group of other asylum seekers—part of the December "migrant surge" that propelled the panties of the U.S. politico-media establishment into a massive bunch. Never mind that the U.S. Chamber of Commerce itself continues to report a distinct "labor shortage" in America: "We have a lot of jobs but not enough workers to fill them. If every unemployed person in the country found a job, we would still have millions of open jobs."[59]

As Isamar and Yurbis later recounted to me, the group was halted on the border by U.S. authorities and a standoff of several days ensued, coming to an end only when people began fainting from lack of food and water. The family was once again separated, and some members were sent to the city of McAllen nearly 500 kilometers away for processing. Just after Christmas, all were loaded onto buses bound for Chicago, one of the U.S. metropolises—along with Washington, D.C., New York City, and a handful of others—that Texas governor Greg Abbott had determined should pay for the Biden administration's "refusal to secure the border." In addition to manically busing asylum seekers to these cities, Abbott also began flying migrants out of Texas by charter plane in December after Chicago cracked down on "rogue" bus operators.

And while the spectacle naturally won the governor points in a state that prides itself on sensational displays of sociopathy, Abbott's vision of an immigration free-for-all on the border failed to account for such things as Biden's deportation of more than 142,000 immigrants in fiscal year 2023—not to mention his administration's decision to waive a slew of federal laws and regulations in order to expand Trump's wall, in contravention of the president's own promises. In a December 2023 dispatch for *The Border Chronicle* titled "The Lucrative Business of 'Border Chaos,'" published right around the time that the Venezuelans of Guanarito were being held in limbo between Piedras Negras and Eagle Pass, investigative journalist Melissa del Bosque observed: "Trump didn't create the border wall, but he'd like Americans to think he did. For nearly 20 years, the border wall economy has metastasized into a multibillion-dollar industry supported by both political parties, an industry that enriches private contractors, military vendors, tech billionaires, and politicians."

Indeed, the U.S. border was alive and well—and not just on the physical U.S. frontier. Since entering the Darién Gap from Colombia, the Venezuelan family had basically contended with one continuous U.S. border replete with life-imperiling obstacles from northern South America to the Rio Grande. As Isamar and Yurbis had been hoping to reach Chicago anyway, they did not complain about free transport on the "Abbott express" and arrived to separate migrant shelters in the city just in time for the new year and their first-ever sighting of snow. Tragedy would strike the family just a month later, but for a moment, at least, they were able to breathe.

On January 13, 2024—the day that Johan, his brother Kelvin, and I arrived in the small northern Colombian port city of Necoclí to catch the boat to the Darién Gap—Colombia's Defense Ministry announced the capture in Necoclí of Pedro Pablo Guzmán, alias "Pelomono," wanted for extradition to the United States for his activities on behalf of the Clan del Golfo, or AGC, the country's reigning drug-trafficking group and neo-paramilitary outfit. The brother-in-law of AGC leader "Chiquito Malo," Pelomono was apprehended at a concert at the Necoclí baseball stadium with the assistance of the U.S. Drug Enforcement Administration, which has since its inception in 1973 somehow never managed to fix the old drug-trafficking problem despite a continuous presence in Colombia and a whole lot of resources expended on the so-called drug war.

With the arrest in 2021 of former AGC chief and Necoclí native Dairo Antonio Úsuga, alias "Otoniel," the group was meant to be on its way to extinction—at least according to the calculations of then-right-wing president Iván Duque, who announced that "the capture of Otoniel is only comparable to the fall of Pablo Escobar" and that "this blow marks the end of the Clan del Golfo." And yet following Otoniel's extradition to the United States, the AGC merely expanded its operations and territorial control, making Duque's comparison to the downfall of the Medellín cartel kingpin valid only insofar as neither "blow" ultimately did jack shit in terms of enfeebling the narco-scape or disrupting the general panorama of violence—one in which the Colombian state itself has of course been a key player since forever. For an idea of how things did not exactly start looking up after Otoniel's capture, consider that 2022 saw 215 killings of social leaders and human rights activists, the highest number ever recorded in Colombia.

To be sure, the United States' simultaneous criminalization of and demand for drugs is largely what ensures narco-trafficking's enduring lucrativeness, just as the country's simultaneous demand for cheap labor and criminalization of migration guarantees big bucks for migrant smugglers. A partial explanation for why the United States has never been overly interested in extirpating the drug trade in spite of its fervent claims to the contrary appears in *Cocaine, Death Squads, and the War on Terror: U.S. Imperialism and Class Struggle in Colombia*, in which scholars Oliver Villar and Drew Cottle offer the following outline of the 1980s, heyday of Pablo Escobar: "The cocaine decade saw the consolidation of the Colombian drug trade as a source of profit for U.S. capital via banks that were established to launder and invest drug money in legitimate U.S. corporations. The United States contended it was at war with drugs and terrorists in Colombia but, in reality, the economic relations between U.S. imperialism and the Colombian narco-bourgeoisie permitted cocaine production to flourish in Colombia, and the cocaine market to expand within the United States and Western Europe."[60]

The drug war also enabled the United States to fling gobs of money at a right-wing state firmly committed to helping violently make the world safe for capitalism—and taking out a whole lot of peasants in the process. In 2000, U.S. lawmakers approved "Plan Colombia," which began with a $1.3 billion injection of mainly military aid—although then-U.S. president Bill Clinton was still not entirely satisfied, complaining in a July 13 statement from Camp David that Congress had "substituted its own judgement for that of the U.S. and Colombian militaries, and provided funding for only 16 of the 30 Blackhawk helicopters requested for the Colombian Army, providing instead funding for 30 Huey II helicopters."

Tragic indeed. But by three years later the United States, now under the enlightened guidance of War on Terror chief George W. Bush, had "funneled more aid to Colombia than into any other country in the hemisphere," as NBC News noted in an October 2003 dispatch titled "'Plan Colombia' Gets Expensive." The South American nation had soared to become the third-largest recipient of U.S. aid in the world, trailing only super-special U.S. allies Israel and Egypt, while Colombian president Álvaro Uribe had promised everyone he would "make Colombia entirely drug free by the end of his term in 2006." Without batting an eye, NBC reminded its audience that the contemporary Colombian conflict had been "shaped by two left-wing groups, the FARC and ELN, battling the government, which has been often supported by right-wing paramilitaries, known as the AUC"—the Autodefensas Unidas de Colombia, or United Self-Defense Forces of Colombia.

NBC News, mind you, is hardly some radical media outlet, and the Colombian military-paramilitary nexus is a long-established fact. Unfortunately for the U.S. narrative, however, the AUC was designated in 2001 as a Foreign Terrorist Organization by the U.S. government, which made it "illegal for persons in the United States or subject to U.S. jurisdiction to provide material support to the AUC." The rationale for the designation, as laid out by secretary of state Colin Powell, was that the AUC had "carried out numerous acts of terrorism, including the massacre of hundreds of civilians [and] the forced displacement of entire villages." Therefore, the United States had decided to "stand with the Government of Colombia against the threats to its democracy from these terrorist groups" by, you know, sending its military billions of dollars for potential use in collaboration with the same groups.[61]

Not that the Colombian military itself did not do a fine job of terrorizing its own citizenry, and by some estimates ten thousand civilians were executed by the army during Uribe's two-term rule of 2002–10, in that long-drawn-out atrocity known as the "false positives" scandal. The killings, which earned their perpetrators bonus pay, holidays, and promotions, were also invoked to warrant yet more military aid to drug war ally Uribe—the same Uribe who appeared on a 1991 U.S. Defense Intelligence Agency report listing the "more important Colombian narco-terrorists contracted by the Colombian narcotic cartels for security, transportation, distribution, collection and enforcement of narcotics operations in both the US and Colombia." Coming in at number eighty-two, the Medellín-born then-Senator Uribe was described as a "close personal friend of Pablo Escobar" and someone who was "dedicated to collaboration with the Medellín cartel at high government levels."[62]

Escobar himself was number seventy-nine, while spot number eighty was occupied by Yair Klein, "retired Israeli army colonel, mercenary and expert in military tactics," who had supplied "advisors to the Medellín cartel to train the cartel paramilitary forces and selected assassin team leaders on how to unleash waves of terrorism in Colombia."[63] Among Klein's trainees was Carlos Castaño, who would go on to cofound, in 1997, none other than the AUC, and who himself spent time in Israel in the early 1980s—where he acknowledged getting the whole *autodefensa*/ self-defense idea in the first place, which was then prominently incorporated into the name of his group. Of course, there is perhaps no one better than the Israelis at casting mass slaughter as "self-defense," a grotesque euphemism the United States has been only too eager to uphold. Israel is also a fine role model in terms of the violent displacement of local populations and the mass production of refugees; ditto for showing just how good perpetual war can be for business. In the case of paramilitarized Colombia, it wasn't just the arms industry that was making a killing; the AUC also dutifully terrorized Colombian communities on behalf of international corporate interests. Just ask Chiquita Brands International, which made protection payments to the designated Foreign Terrorist Organization and was judicially busted accordingly, or the Alabama-based Drummond coal company, the biggest coal exporter in Colombia. In 2007, Drummond went on civil trial in Birmingham for allegedly helping to finance the

AUC, which had assassinated three union leaders for mine workers in 2001. In this case, the company was acquitted.

Speaking of business, in 2008—coincidentally the very year the "false positives" scandal broke—Israel became a "large supplier of military aid and technology to Colombia," as Villar and Cottle note in *Cocaine, Death Squads, and the War on Terror.*[64] Granted, the arrangement would later be complicated when Gustavo Petro, Colombia's first leftist president, objected to Israel's launching of genocide in the Gaza Strip in 2023. But for a while there all was copasetic, and in June 2013 the Israeli newspaper *Haaretz* ran a story on its meeting in Jerusalem with Uribe's successor Juan Manuel Santos, whom they reported was "proud" to have his country called "The Israel of Latin America" and had taken it "as a compliment when Hugo Chavez compared Colombia to Israel." Having served as defense minister under Uribe, Santos naturally already had plenty of blood on his hands—but also enjoyed the Israeli-esque advantage of being able to claim he was fighting "terrorists."

By this time the AUC had been officially demobilized, meaning the group had disbanded only to reincarnate in other forms such as the *Águilas Negras*, or Black Eagles, whose contributions to society Amelia and I superficially witnessed while hitchhiking through Colombia in 2009. In the southern Colombian department of Putumayo, for example, villagers reported that the *Águilas Negras* had been posting fliers threatening to kill prostitutes and anyone else who went outdoors after 10 P.M.; other signage in the village comprised advertisements courtesy of the U.S. Agency for International Development reminding folks not to grow coca and to grow other things instead. The formation of the *Águilas Negras* came about under the supervision of Vicente Castaño, brother of Carlos and cofounder of the AUC, who along with other former AUC commanders also presided over the founding in the northern Urabá region of what would become the AGC—the Autodefensas Gaitanistas de Colombia, with the Israeli-inherited "*autodefensa*" terminology going strong. The AGC has boasted a million other names, as well, and in early 2024 its members made it known that they now wanted to be called the Ejército Gaitanista de Colombia, or the Gaitanist Army of Colombia.

Rather than a traditional paramilitary force operating in symbiosis with the military, the Clan del Golfo often counteracts and supplants the government. A 2023 essay in the Colombian news outlet *Vorágine* quotes Luis Fernando Trejos, a professor at Colombia's Universidad del Norte and an expert on the country's armed conflict, on how it's erroneous to view the AGC as a "simple extension of the AUC," first and foremost because the Gaitanistas are not a counterinsurgent group. Another common error, according to Trejos, is to categorize the AGC as "narcos pure and simple" given that in the territories under its control the organization "fulfills exclusive functions of the state," including the administration of justice: "What does the resolution of problems over property boundaries between neighbors or domestic violence issues have to do with [control of] the cocaine market?" In the town of Unguía inside the Darién Gap, *Vorágine* notes that the AGC controls "various aspects of daily life, including such simple acts as moving from one place to another"—which goes not only for local residents but also for migrants, whose movement through the jungle generates additional millions for the group.[65]

In August 2024 the Petro government would authorize the initiation of dialogue with the AGC, including clan leader "Chiquito Malo," himself a former member of the AUC. But as of my arrival in Colombia in January the country's forever war seemingly continued apace, with the Medellín-based *El Colombiano* newspaper reporting a 275 percent increase in homicides that month in Urabá—a phenomenon some experts had attributed to the DEA-assisted capture of "Pelomono" in Necoclí and related maneuvers by the state.[66] It is lamentably fitting, to say the least, that the Colombian region serving as the gateway to the jungle—a jungle the U.S. media have taken to crassly referring to as a "highway for migrants" bound for the United States—has itself long been characterized by mass displacement and forced migration, much of it a product of U.S.-backed militarized capitalism.

I arrived in Medellín on January 10 by plane from Panama City to meet up with Johan and his twenty-five-year-old brother Kelvin, who were due to arrive by bus from Cúcuta, the Colombian city on the Venezuelan border where Kelvin resided with their father. Kelvin had not set foot in Venezuela in more than three years following a jail stint, which had been occasioned by an infraction summarized for me by Johan as "stealing something but not from like a poor person, from like a rich ballsucker." Until recently Kelvin had worked construction jobs in Cúcuta and environs, but the work had gradually dried up; he therefore jumped at the chance to earn some extra cash helping to escort his brother's random gringa into the jungle.

I had flown to Panama after spending the Christmas holidays with my mom in D.C., where I had gone about ordering everything Amazon thought I should order for an excursion into the wilderness: cheap tent, rain ponchos, beef jerky, headlamps, water purifying straw, cell phone power bank. I also invested in super-toxic mosquito repellent after reading, in Spanish, the rather excruciatingly long-winded *Explorations of the Isthmuses of Panama and Darién in 1876, 1877 and 1878* by the French engineer and naval officer M. A. Reclus, who wrote of the latter isthmus:

> But there are mosquitoes, and in such a quantity that even my pen is colliding with these abominable insects, which the Semites consider to be sons of Beelzebub, prince of demons, and which I will only talk about now so as to not have to return to this maddening matter [*Spoiler alert: Reclus would be back with plenty more to say about the abominable insects later on*.]. . . . The story goes that Simeon Stylite spent 40 years atop a pillar striving to earn his place in heaven; however, it is certain that, had he imposed such a penance on himself living in any of the regions of the Darién, the rabid hordes that are now assaulting

and biting us from every direction would have caused him to come down much sooner.[67]

Apart from the mosquito repellent, most of my Amazon-acquired items would not be utilized in the end and would be donated to Johan along with the machetes purchased in Necoclí for his subsequent crossing of the Darién Gap. While in Panama I made a quick trip to Metetí to visit Belisario and family and to check up on the progress the Panamanian authorities were making in their ostensible crackdown on migration, the only discernible change on the ground being that my bus back to Panama City was stopped five times for inspection by the *Servicio Nacional de Fronteras* (SENAFRONT). The government-organized migrant buses to Costa Rica were still operating as usual, and on the side of the Pan-American Highway in Metetí large letters spelling "SENAFRONT" had been erected in case visitors wanted a photo op with the name of Panama's National Border Service.

In Panama City I stayed once again at the Quarry Heights residence of Canadian Émile, who was in Canada, and practiced for the jungle by traipsing up and down Ancón Hill, all the while channeling my anxiety, à la my father, into baseless medical auto-diagnoses. So it was that I came down not only with lymphoma but with throat cancer, as well, and tried to reason with myself that I shouldn't be so scared of the jungle if I was dying anyway. I also spent many hours seated at Émile's dining room table conferring by WhatsApp with Yurbis, who had taken over communications from Isamar, at the migrant shelter in Chicago, where she would stay for several months before the American dream took flight and landed her a job at a Butterball poultry processing plant in North Carolina. Yurbis assured me that the whole family would be praying for me and sent me some last-minute reminders: make Johan carry everything, harden your heart because you're going to see a lot of suffering, and before you go to the jungle eat a *bandeja paisa* in Medellín—the iconic Colombian dish consisting of sausage, pork rinds, egg, beans, rice, and a bunch of other light stuff.

Yurbis handed the phone off to her eight-year-old son Daniel, who, sounding downright chipper, informed me that there was "nothing to be afraid of" in the selva and that he had liked the selva just fine. He then revised his glowing review to acknowledge that he had in fact been scared of thieves: "But that was the only thing that scared me. Well, that and the river. And also the animals, because there are snakes like the *mapaná* [pit viper]." From the background came Yurbis's voice: "And the *muertos*"—to which Daniel replied, "No, not the *muertos*, because I didn't see any." Daniel's thirteen-year-old sister Valeria was up next and explained that her brother hadn't seen any *muertos* because any time a *muerto* was encountered the family had distracted him or covered his eyes. For her part, Valeria appeared to have been less troubled by the physical corpses than by the "lost souls" she said were wandering the jungle.

My departure to Medellín on January 10 nearly didn't happen, as shortly prior to leaving for the airport I received a notification from Copa Airlines that their planes were grounded on account of the Boeing/Alaska Airlines incident—a first-world travel problem, yes, but I did need to get to Colombia, which was so close if not for the jungle standing in the way. After some scrambling on the Internet and high blood pressure, I was booked on the heretofore unheard of Colombian airline Wingo, which departed not out of Panama City's Tocumen International but rather out of the tiny Panamá Pacífico Airport, also known as Balboa Airport after everyone's favorite Spanish conquistador and located on the site of the former Howard Air Force Base, where my grandfather had resided for a time.

Johan and Kelvin's arrival in Medellín was meanwhile delayed for fifteen hours by an accident somewhere past the city of Bucaramanga that made the road impassable—a phenomenon Amelia and I had grown most familiar with while hitchhiking through Colombia for a month in 2009, when countless hours were spent immobile in the cabs of cargo trucks whose drivers had wandered off in search of food or entertainment, abandoning their rides in the middle of the thoroughfare with the knowledge that no one was going anywhere anytime soon. While I waited for Johan and Kelvin, I went over such final pressing first-world matters as whether I should take my nighttime tooth guard into the jungle and paid a visit to Medellín's botanical gardens, where I witnessed my first-ever duel between male iguanas while a female iguana went about her business. Commentary was provided by Colombian onlookers, one of whom narrated the female iguana's thoughts: "Go ahead and fight, you idiots; I'll just be over here."

The brothers arrived on the night of January 11 and set about devouring everything that could be devoured. I hadn't seen Johan since Madrid three and a half months earlier, and we spent a full night and day in blissful harmony—with Johan performing his charming impersonation of the Medellín accent—before resuming our modus operandi of bickering over things like whether Las Vegas was a place anyone should want to go to. This was my first encounter with Kelvin, who unlike Johan had not converted his brown hair to blond and who bore a large tattoo across his chest depicting his and Johan's niece, who had died as a baby in Caracas. Kelvin was initially reserved with me and barely spoke the night of their arrival, but this changed quickly the next day when instead of preparing for the following day's journey to Necoclí, we got sidetracked drinking Águila beer in Plaza Botero, named for the Medellín-born sculptor. As per Yurbis's insistence we also consumed *bandeja paisa*, but most of the day was spent in one of those distinctly Latin American watering holes where the beer costs almost the same as in the supermarket and the patrons are separated from the alcohol stock and the server by jail-like bars.

From our plastic table we had a direct view of the bulbous horse ass belonging to one of Botero's sculptures featured in the plaza, and I did my best to comply with the request by Johan and Kelvin's mother Nelvis that I continuously send her photos of her sons such that she might upload them to her WhatsApp status. While Nelvis was still unclear as to what precisely we were all doing in Colombia, she was certain that whatever it was, God was looking after us. A few hundred rounds into the Águila, we received a free round courtesy of a Colombian woman who apparently had the hots for Kelvin, until she invited herself to sit with us and found out he was Venezuelan. She then dedicated herself to conversing with me and decided it would be helpful to warn me not to go into the jungle because she would never see me again.

The bus to Necoclí departed at 8 A.M. from the Medellín bus terminal, which was decorated with signage encouraging folks to migrate legally. Once we had boarded, the after-effects of Águila were felt even more acutely thanks to an incessant beeping that occurred approximately every seven seconds for the duration of the nine-hour ride. With a shrug the bus attendant explained that they had tried everything but that the beeping could not be deactivated, which at least meant that I had plenty of mathematical projects to keep me busy as I calculated how many beeps the bus attendant had to endure per day, week, and so on. As we left the city behind and curved up into the mist of rural Antioquia—the Colombian department encompassing both Medellín and Necoclí—the woman in front of Johan and me commenced puking into a plastic bag, and I was reminded of the last time I had traveled this simultaneously nausea-inducing and gloriously scenic route in the back of a pickup truck with Amelia. More Colombian mountain curves had been navigated in the cab of a fuel truck emblazoned with the warning *Peligro* across the back, which had not stopped its driver from careening around said curves.

Then came the gradual descent and, several thousand beeps later, we were flying past banana plantations as we neared the Gulf of Urabá. The bus made a stop in the town of Apartadó, located just down the road from the Peace Community of San José de Apartadó, where Amelia and I had been hosted for a week in 2009 after reading about the community in Forrest Hylton's book *Evil Hour in Colombia* and just showing up. Founded in 1997 on a commitment to rejecting cooperation with all armed actors in the region—military, paramilitary, and guerilla alike—the Peace Community had as of the time of our visit suffered no fewer than

184 assassinations out of a population of around 1,500. Responsibility for the overwhelming majority of the crimes was attributed to the military-paramilitary alliance, with the Revolutionary Armed Forces of Colombia (FARC) blamed for a significantly lesser share. The Peace Community dedicated itself to the collective cultivation of miniature bananas and cacao, among other activities, which for a week also included attending to two uninvited visitors, one from Washington, D.C., and the other from Rzeszów, Poland. Especial patience was extended by community cofounder María Brígida González, a woman with a pair of grey braids and mud boots, whose fifteen-year-old daughter Eliseña had been murdered in her sleep in 2005 by members of the Colombian army's 17th Brigade and marked down as a FARC casualty. As María Brígida summed it up, the objective of such attacks on the Peace Community was to "sow terror" in order to displace the community and facilitate corporate exploitation of the area's abundant resources; in Colombia, after all, peace was not conducive to business.

At some point between Apartadó and the coastal city of Turbo—which along with Necoclí was another jumping-off point for the Darién Gap—I overheard the elderly Afro-Colombian man behind me tell another passenger that he was from Capurganá. Having already banished Johan across the aisle after determining that the beeping was surely somehow fundamentally his fault, I contorted myself in the seat to interrogate the man, who was returning from his ex-wife's funeral in Medellín, for which his various daughters living in Barcelona had also flown in. The man had lived in Panama City for twenty-five years, he told me, but now he was content at home in Capurganá, which despite being technically located within the Darién Gap had not inspired him to venture into the jungle: "The selva is for young people." As it turned out, I was not the only eavesdropper on the bus, and the Colombian man in front of me then swiveled around to advertise the services of his friend Wilson, who would take me into the jungle for cheaper than anyone else. The man from Capurganá gave me a slight shake of the head to register his assessment of this option, but three Venezuelans seated farther back on the bus promptly moved forward to confer with Wilson's honorary booking agent. They descended with him in Turbo, which boasted two consecutive social clubs named Sinaloa—like the Mexican state and eponymous cartel—and Culiacán, the capital of Sinaloa.

The Afro-Colombian of Capurganá also got off in Turbo, while Johan, Kelvin, and I continued on to Necoclí, the plan still being to repeat the Necoclí-Acandí route that Johan had taken the previous year. Just before arriving in Necoclí the bus was stopped at a checkpoint and boarded by an overzealous police officer, who went about lifting Johan's and Kelvin's shirts and extensively probing their groin areas, whereupon I announced with my best gringo self-righteousness: "They're with me." The officer raised his hands in mock surrender—"Oh, they're with you!"—and retreated with a wink, leaving us to cover in peace the remaining distance to Necoclí, where the weather was reminiscent of a furnace and the scenery resembled "a border town," as Kelvin declared. As we stood in the blazing dust on the side of the road where the bus had deposited us—the beeping having been seemingly permanently implanted in our brains—Johan embarked on a trip down memory lane to the night he had spent in Necoclí with El Mono, Felipe, and Andrés, and I embarked on plans to submerge myself in the Gulf of Urabá as quickly as possible.

I had booked two nights at a Necoclí hostel to give Johan and Kelvin time to obtain machetes and a substance called *creolina*, which Johan insisted was essential for repelling snakes. We also needed to sort out what we thought was going to be boat passage to Acandí but ended up being to Capurganá, instead, the reason being that the staff at the boat company's office responded with raised eyebrows when I said I was going on holiday to Acandí with my Venezuelan boyfriend and his brother. Certainly we'd have a better time in Capurganá, they said, as Acandí wasn't much of a holiday spot, to which I had no choice but to agree wholeheartedly and pay for the tickets. In the end our destination mattered little, as the jungle was equally reachable by either location, but migrants were not generally permitted to purchase tickets to Acandí or Capurganá at the normal tourist price and either had to drastically overpay for the boat or, more commonly by now, pay for the whole jungle-crossing package right there in Necoclí, at more than $300 a pop. The office staff inspected with a good amount of skepticism Johan and Kelvin's travel documents, which consisted respectively of a Venezuelan passport bearing an expired Colombian entry stamp and a Venezuelan identity card, putting them pretty solidly in the "migrant" category. I made such a nuisance of myself chattering about maritime conditions and safety protocol on the boat, however, that eventually a nod was given and tickets were in hand.

The beach and sidewalks of Necoclí hosted all manner of tents, hammocks, sleeping mats, and cardboard boxes where migrants from an array of nations waited days, weeks, or months to gather the fare for onward passage. Those with the means stayed in hotels or rented houses, as was the case with a group of Haitians opposite our hostel, who with their loudspeaker provided a welcome musical backdrop to perishing in the heat. Johan and Kelvin took turns making arepas and taking photos in front of the "TE ❤ NECOCLÍ" letters adorning the seaside, which gave the SENAFRONT display in Metetí a run for its money and came complete with the encouraging addendum, *Tú perteneces aquí*—"You belong here."

This was the same seaside where, the previous October, New York City's Democratic mayor Eric Adams had done his best to discourage migrants from trying to travel to the United States because, he said, the going was rough "on the streets of New York."[68] To be sure, while everyone might have belonged in Necoclí—at least per the hospitable sign—there was not a warm welcome waiting for folks in America. There might, however, have been a bus to New York courtesy of Texas governor Abbott, who while addressing the 2024 National Rifle Association convention in Dallas would promise to carry on with his migrant busing program because "Mayor Adams needs something to do."[69] Necoclí was also, incidentally, the port where in the early 1980s Pablo Escobar received his first batch of exotic animals purchased for $2 million from a zoo in none other than Dallas, which he had personally visited with an eye to populating his Hacienda Nápoles. In her book *Mrs Escobar: My Life with Pablo*, Victoria Eugenia Henao describes the zoo trip as the "happiest one he ever took," Pablo being "so delighted with everything that he even agreed to climb up on the back of one of the elephants, where he remained for almost ten minutes." Then it was time to arrange the animals' southward migration: "Two weeks after returning from Dallas, my husband organised the first trip to bring the largest group of animals into the country. They arrived via a rented ship that docked in the port city of Necoclí, on the Caribbean coast 250 miles from Medellín. From there the animals were transported by truck to Nápoles in what turned out to be a complicated operation. Concerned about how long and risky the retrieval trip had been, Pablo decided to switch to secret flights."[70]

So it was that four hippopotamuses were able to travel between continents in greater style and comfort than the average contemporary undocumented human. In the very least, the secretly flown hippos did not have to suffer the vertebral implosion that attended maritime navigation of the Gulf of Urabá, an effect of boat crashing against waves. When Johan, Kelvin, and I set sail from Necoclí on the morning of January 15, the captain informed us that the waves today were "nothing," in which case I would not wish waves that were "something" on anyone's spine. We had arrived early at the dock and set about waiting with the rest of the international crowd for our names to be called; although it was technically low season for migration, one boat after another was packed to the brim with life jacket–clad passengers, the majority of them migrants but with some vacationing Colombian families thrown into the mix, as well. Vendors sold arepas and waterproof cell phone pouches as well as heavy-duty black plastic bags, in which personal belongings were secured for placement beneath the seats of the vessel.

I had left my computer along with most of my other crap with the owner of the hostel because, after much contemplation of the logistics of the Darién Gap trip, it had been decided that, instead of continuing through to Panama, we would exit the Gap from the Colombian side and return to Medellín via Necoclí. There were various reasons for this, including that I was not traveling with any sort of journalistic or other permission, and that I was not overly interested in seeing what would happen if I entered Panama at Bajo Chiquito as a "migrant" and then tried to fly out of Panama City with no Panamanian entry stamp in my passport. There was also the matter of my columnist gig with *Al Jazeera*, from which I could not afford to take time off and which prevented me from straying too far from my computer for more than a couple of days. As there was no way in hell I was taking the computer into the jungle, the most logical course of action seemed to be to leave it in Necoclí.

On top of all of that, I did not want to make Johan and Kelvin do a round-trip tour of the jungle, walking all the way to Panama and back with double the opportunities for misfortune. Most importantly of all, perhaps, I was simply a coward—and I really, really, really did not want to be raped. To be sure, it speaks volumes to the grotesque state of the world that some of us have the option to decide whether or not we wish to put ourselves in a position where the chances of being sexually violated are inordinately high. For countless women, children, and men, violent penetration is par for the migratory course—and in the case of the Darién Gap, nearly all sexual aggression takes place on the Panamanian side. On the Colombian side, it seems, such violence has been largely brought under control in the interest of business, not that this makes it a walk in the park. Granted, plenty of American journalists have crossed the Darién Gap in its entirety, but this has generally been done with Panamanian government or other protection. In his book *Another Day of Life*, which deals with the 1975 outbreak of civil war in Angola, the late Polish journalist

Ryszard Kapuściński opined: "As I see it, it's wrong to write about people without living through at least a little of what they are living through."[71] And while Kapuściński of course lived through a little and much more of what other people did, I myself could not come to grips with the idea of totally relinquishing control over my body, and hoped I did not need to be raped to tell the story.

From Necoclí we crashed through the waves for approximately two hours, with me digging my nails into Johan and Kelvin on either side of me and lamenting the one-liter bottle of Aguardiente Antioqueño I had allowed them to purchase the previous night. The boat stopped first in Acandí, where a portion of the passengers were hustled off the vessel with their black plastic bags while the woman receiving them on the dock loudly forbade the taking of pictures. Then it was back out to sea and on to the turquoise waters of Capurganá, flanked by lush vegetation—a paradoxically idyllic backdrop, no doubt, to the entrance to the "green hell." Staggering off the boat, we extricated ourselves from our life jackets and collected our plastic bags, while a greeter on the dock welcomed the new arrivals and assured us Capurganá was "totally safe"—albeit without electricity for the past week, a situation that would not resolve itself in the near future.

I had reserved a room for one night in a hotel overlooking the sea, where we were required to enter our names, ID numbers, and professions into a registration book; as a writer I was the least original entry, but Johan got to be a model and Kelvin a singer. Capurganá was small and loud, and at a table in the center of the village by the dock there was a rowdy game of dominoes that appeared to be perennially underway. There was also a cosmetic presence of Colombian police, who could occasionally be seen demanding to look in someone's backpack or riding around on their motorcycles taking pictures of themselves in action, presumably to submit to their superiors as proof that they were working. I was accustomed to this sort of behavior in Zipolite, where the police were known to drive up and down the beach photographing each other on their all-terrain vehicles and drinking beer concealed in plastic cups while the local underworld conducted periodic assassinations in broad daylight. In Capurganá, migrant trafficking operations took place in plain view, and I watched from the window of our hotel room as a group of what seemed to be Bangladeshi and Haitian migrants were paraded from the dock past the hotel to the auto rickshaws that would transport them the short distance to the *albergue*, or shelter—the last stop before the jungle.

Much has been written about the role of social media in migration via the Darién Gap, with *The New York Times*, for example, highlighting the "trafficking operations that ply their services openly on Facebook and TikTok." Contending that social media has "become a powerful amplifier of the Darién route" and that "thousands are drawn to the dangerous crossing through social media posts," the *Times* cites posts created by "swindlers claiming that the route is not that difficult or even that the United States is offering sanctuary to certain nationalities." All of this has fueled the "enormous flood of migrants through the Darién [that] is feeding a growing political problem" in the United States, with the Darién Gap becoming "a traffic jam."[72] For its part, the Associated Press suggests that the more than half a million migrants that crossed the Darién Gap in 2023 were "enabled by social media and Colombian organized crime," which had converted the "once nearly impenetrable" jungle into a "speedy but still treacherous highway."[73]

Granted, social media influence with regard to the phenomenon of migration is to be entirely expected given that social media has effectively become a substitute for the world itself these days. But facile implications of causality downplay the role of more substantive factors, such as that U.S. policies have helped render swaths of the earth unlivable. Once again, that scribbled line from the notes I made in the Siglo XXI migrant jail in Tapachula comes to mind: "Cubans say no one leaves their country and walks thru selva for a week if they don't have to"—to which I might add that no one walks through the selva for a week just because TikTok tells them to. Relatedly, millions of people somehow managed to make their way to Ellis Island without the enablement of either social media or Colombian organized crime, which just goes to underscore that human beings migrate when they perceive the need to migrate.

That said, we would quickly ascertain in Capurganá that Colombian organized crime was very, let's say, organized. After spending the rest of the day of our arrival swimming at the beach—where Johan consumed some elaborate concoction prepared in a hollowed-out pineapple, Kelvin exclaimed over the fish in the sea, and I felt old and motherly—we checked out of our hotel early on the morning of January 16. The receptionist kindly agreed to hold on to my passport and cell phone and refrained from asking questions. Turning left out of the hotel entrance, we walked a few hundred meters to a waiting auto rickshaw, whose driver also refrained from asking questions and simply motioned for us to climb in. This was the complimentary transport to the *albergue*, where we would soon enough be extorted for all we were worth.

Johan and Kelvin were carrying most of the crap I had ordered on Amazon plus five liters of water each, while I was in charge of a backpack stuffed with beef jerky, energy bars, and chocolate that had long ago melted. Johan also had all of the money and the designated picture-taking phone, which had to be utilized surreptitiously after a ban on photos was announced and which meant I ended up with a lot of selfies of Johan in the Darién Gap. I was once again sporting my Palestine soccer shirt—the same shirt I had been wearing when Johan and I met in Bajo Chiquito almost a year earlier—this time with black Adidas pants with neon green stripes that had already been disintegrating when I had bought them at a used clothing store in Tbilisi, Georgia. Johan had forbidden me from wearing the sunglasses that were normally welded to my head, and when we arrived at the *albergue* he snapped a photo of me and declared approvingly that I looked like a real live migrant.

The *albergue*, a space built to accommodate hundreds of people, was open-air minus a covered section and was almost empty when we entered, with only scattered groups of migrants sitting in plastic chairs and on the ground. A few men who appeared to be employed as guides were conversing with the disparate groups; I overheard one of them assure a family with an infant that it was "only five minutes" to the Panamanian border, while another family was told it was four hours. The walls of the *albergue* bore leftover holiday murals—with reindeer, a sleigh, a tree, and wishes for a merry Christmas and happy new year—along with a painting of an Indigenous girl in a hat and another of people crossing a river. One of the plastic chairs held a snoozing cat, and a chicken with most of its feathers missing made the rounds.

In the center of the roofed portion of the space a sign hung from the ceiling featuring "general information" in both Spanish and English. The latter version read:

"Darién jungle crossing Colombia—Panamá
'Walker there is no path, the path is made by walking'
Generating more hope, to achieve the American Dream"

Small Colombian and Panamanian flags were painted on the sign, while a much larger U.S. flag occupied its rightmost section. Arranged on top of the sign were a pair of rainboots and four individual children's shoes. Lest migrants underestimate the literary connoisseurship of their traffickers, it should be noted that the quote appearing as the centerpiece of the "general information" was taken from a poem by the Spaniard Antonio Machado, who died in exile in the south of France in 1939, the same year Francisco Franco assumed the dictatorship of Spain. According to the *El Mundo* newspaper, as per his own instructions Machado was buried with some Spanish dirt he had carried with him across the border. His mother died three days later.[74]

As I had been advised to keep my mouth shut to the extent possible, Johan and Kelvin were dispatched to speak with a Colombian man in flip-flops who strolled into the *albergue* emanating authority. They returned to report that it would be $280 per person to enter the jungle and that an identifying document was required, which put me in a bit of a fix. When the flip-flopped man strolled over to collect the documents, Johan handed his and Kelvin's Venezuelan IDs over and announced that I had lost mine, prompting the man to ask me what I had to identify myself with. "My face?" proved to be an acceptable answer, our money was taken, and I was escorted up a flight of stairs to a room where the flip-flopped man handed a portion of the funds over to a woman at a desk. This woman took my name down on a piece of paper as Maria Velen Hernandez and asked for the number of my missing document but not the country to which it pertained, so I recited my U.S. passport number and that was the end of that.

Back down the stairs we went, and the man affixed two bands to our wrists to indicate that we had paid—a much less complicated undertaking in Johan and Kelvin's case as every millimeter of wrist space was not already taken up by other bracelets. One of the bands was purple and imprinted with the word "Final"; the other was yellow and imprinted with a series of frog faces. I asked the man if the jungle was safe, to which he responded, "*Gracias a Dios* it is safe" and went on to claim that we would be led by Colombian guides the whole time and stay in *albergues* "just like this one." Unable to help myself, I then asked him where two Yemeni-seeming men who had just turned up were from, to which he responded: "I have no idea; go ask them."

When I interrupted the men they were huddled over a cell phone inspecting a map of the Darién. Looking up with a smile, they confirmed in English that they were indeed from Yemen and endorsed my Palestine shirt as "very good." The men were not sure if they were scared, they told me, as they had never done this before and didn't know what to expect—although it surely couldn't be worse than, you know, the war in Yemen. Evidently registering my own terror, they set about reckoning that all would be fine in the jungle and volunteered: "If you need anything, we are here." They were not there for much longer, however, as before the group to which Johan, Kelvin, and I had been assigned was called, a guide whisked the two Yemenis off to commence their chance at "Generating more hope, to achieve the American Dream."

While the United States has never officially been at war with Yemen, it is another one of those places where successive U.S. administrations have gone about inflicting terror out of sight and out of mind of the general U.S. public—and always with the alibi, of course, of "fighting terrorism." America's covert action program in Yemen was launched in 2002 under the auspices of George W. Bush but only took off for real in 2009 under Barack Obama, who, as the London-based Bureau of Investigative Journalism has noted, "embraced the US drone programme, overseeing more strikes in his first year than Bush carried out in his entire presidency." Overall, Obama would preside over "ten times more air strikes in the covert war on terror" in Yemen, Somalia, and Pakistan than Bush had, killing between 384 and 807 civilians in those three countries per the bureau's calculations—none of which stopped the Obama administration from gushing that drone strikes were so "exceptionally surgical and precise."[75] Among the "surgical" victims were twelve people killed in rural Yemen in December 2013 when a U.S. drone unleashed four Hellfire missiles on a wedding procession.

Things got even more exceptional when Donald Trump took over as commander in chief of America, and the bureau reported more U.S. strikes on Yemen in Trump's first one hundred days as president in 2017 than in all of the previous two years combined. Shortly after Trump decided to exempt Yemen from the Obama-implemented White House Rules on Targeted Killing, which meant that the military now got "to authorise strikes without running them through the White House security bureaucracy first," a bureau field investigation indicated that at least twenty-five civilians had died in a January 29 U.S. operation involving multiple air strikes.[76] Meanwhile, the United States didn't even have to do the bulk of the dirty work in Yemen itself, boasting as it did such upstanding allies as Saudi Arabia and the United Arab Emirates, ever on call to do things like blow up buses full of Yemeni schoolchildren with U.S.-supplied bombs. This particular achievement in the fight against terror killed forty children and eleven adults in northwest Yemen in August 2018—the same year the Associated Press identified at least five Emirati-run prisons in Yemen "where security forces use sexual torture to brutalize and break inmates" and the year after the AP's documentation of at least eighteen secret Emirati-affiliated prisons-cum-torture centers where the United States was also known to interrogate detainees.[77] Add to that the Saudi-led blockade of Yemen that was imposed in 2017 and that kept the country firmly on the brink of famine, and you start to understand why two Yemeni guys might have found it necessary to travel halfway around the world and walk through the selva for a week. Just a week prior to our meeting at the *albergue* of Capurganá, Joe Biden had launched the United States' latest unofficial war on Yemen by authorizing airstrikes against the country in response to efforts by Yemen's Houthis to disrupt Red Sea shipping in solidarity with Palestine.

After a wait of an hour or so at the *albergue*, our group was summoned for departure. We were more than twenty people in all, everyone Venezuelan except for Maria Velen Hernandez and a woman from Bogotá and her son. As we were herded out of the gate, several auto rickshaws pulled up packed with Chinese passengers, some of the girls in skirts and sandals—a wardrobe choice that only made sense later when I was informed by a guide that the Chinese were bound for Carreto, Panama, by sea, one of the pricier routes that entailed far less walking. Our next step involved more rickshaws, this time for a fee of a few dollars; those not wishing to pay had to walk to the edge of Capurganá, where the real walking began. We were accompanied by an assortment of guides and porters, some of them in colored T-shirts bearing the words *"Apoyo al migrante"*—migrant support.

In a September 2023 article titled "'A Ticket to Disney'? Politicians Charge Millions to Send Migrants to U.S.," *The New York Times* reported that a certain Fundación Social Nueva Luz del Darién, or New Light Darién Foundation, had materialized on the Colombian side of the jungle to oversee the trans-Darién migrant trajectory: "The foundation has hired more than 2,000 local guides and backpack carriers, organized in teams with numbered T-shirts of varying colors—lime green, butter yellow, sky blue—like members of an amateur soccer league." Tied up in the multimillion-dollar enterprise were local politicos and businessfolk, while Colombian president Gustavo Petro was said to estimate that the Clan del Golfo—the outfit ultimately running the show—raked in some $30 million annually in its cut of the migratory proceeds (small change, perhaps, compared to the billions it makes from drug trafficking). An investigation by the *Vorágine* news outlet that came on the heels of the *Times* piece found that money accumulated by the New Light Darién Foundation was in turn utilized to fund the—ultimately successful—mayoral election campaign of the half-brother of one of the New Light leaders, a reliable recipe for a self-sustaining cycle.[78] The foundation managed the *albergues* in Capurganá and Acandí and tended to cast its work in a humanitarian light, as Johan, Kelvin, and I would soon note when one of the guides informed us that migration was going to happen whether anyone liked it or not and that at least the guides on the Colombian side were making it "safe."

In the back of the noncomplimentary rickshaws we passed Capurganá's tiny airport, a "Muscle Gym," and a couple of other landmarks of civilization before being deposited at a creek, where the rickshaws turned back, the trek commenced, and I found myself behind a Venezuelan man with a bag emblazoned with some inspirational words in English: "Make memorable moments." By the time we got to the second creek I had given up on trying not to get water in my sneakers and walked the rest of the nine or so hours with wet feet. I tried to make small talk with one of the guides about the coordinates of the next *albergue*, whereupon he announced somewhat belligerently that I sounded like a gringa. I pleaded Palestinian-ness, indicating my shirt, and was thereafter referred to with a roll of the eyes as "Palestina."

This particular guide warned us not to take pictures of him or his colleagues, one of whom then introduced a blanket ban on photography. Porters continuously offered to carry bags, and two horses were also available to mount—first for a fee of eighty dollars, then forty when there were no takers, and finally twenty. Conveniently, the handlers of the horses did not specify the length of the trajectory to which payment corresponded. This ended up being only to the top of a steep and winding ascent just beyond Capurganá, which while grueling enough in the punishing heat was a fraction of the day's exertion. A Venezuelan woman with a crying infant broke down and paid for the horse only to be forcibly dismounted shortly thereafter, and spent the rest of the day visibly on the verge of fainting.

One of the porters, who was carrying several backpacks from different customers and who all the way up the ascent tried to persuade Johan to trade his fake designer sneakers for the man's own rubber boots, told us at the summit that he had once done this trip seven times in a single day. Business was currently in a post-holiday slump, and the previous day a mere two hundred migrants had set out from Capurganá, but things would pick up soon. Near the beginning of the hill was a shack selling refreshments, where our group paused to rest and Johan and Kelvin shared a Gatorade for exactly twice the normal price. The climb was facilitated by a newish road that had been plowed through the wilderness and that, while not paved, perhaps visually approximated the migrant "highway" the media had taken to crowing about. The plowed stretch would end soon enough, but for the moment Johan observed that this was "fuck, way easier" than the route from Acandí.

At the top of the hill the porters and horse handlers collected their payments and prepared to return to Capurganá, while I assumed that this was where the "*Apoyo al migrante*" terminated and the robbing and raping kicked off. As it turned out, we were not being abandoned yet, and the token female guide—we'll call her Kelly—informed us that she would be leading us to the next *albergue*, still several hours away. Kelly was a robust twenty-eight-year-old Afro-Colombian woman whose gleaming white sneakers appeared to repel mud and dust. She went from joking with the other guides about how she was leaving for "los United" to find herself a gringo to joking with the men in our group about which of them she was going to marry—the answer being none of them since none of them were gringos.

Off we went into the forest to slide down a mountain of mud that was tricky enough in the present dry season conditions but that did offer some arresting views. In a feat of unusual coordination I managed to avoid any catastrophic falls myself, but I did extricate a young Venezuelan girl named Kamila from the puddle in which she had landed prostrate. Kamila had already been in decidedly gloomy spirits, which were not helped by the layer of mud now caked to her, but her outlook improved when we once again reached relatively flat land and passed through some mid-jungle farms populated by cows and donkeys. "All that's missing here," Kamila declared, "are sheep."

Kelly gradually lost her patience on account of the group's slow pace and repeated requests for rest stops and lectured us that at this rate we would never get anywhere in the jungle or in life. At one break by a river, an older Venezuelan woman traveling alone asked her compatriots if today counted as one of the three days she had been told it would take to cross to Panama and was informed that, no, today didn't count. From her position splayed on the grass came the response: "Coño de su madre"—literally "cunt of your mother." Kelly meanwhile sought to expedite movement by appropriating the crying infant from the near-fainting mother and carrying the baby herself the rest of the way, while also providing such important tips for our safety and well-being as: "Don't put your heads in the river after sweating because you could die." Johan and Kelvin shared some of our stock of energy bars with the group, the consensus being that they were "weird."

Some five hours after leaving Capurganá we arrived at the next *albergue*, which was not so much a structure as a small, covered area where folks could jostle for a space to put their tents and where food, water, and Internet were available for a not inconsiderable fee. From there it was a straight shot to the Panamanian border, we were told brusquely by the man in charge, and we were expected to be up and out by six in the morning; furthermore, there were no more *albergues* after this, so it was recommended to rest up. Kelvin was in the process of erecting our tent when I noticed Kelly retreating in the direction of Capurganá, and, spontaneously assessing the situation and my utter lack of balls, I ran after her, the *albergue* man close behind me. Since the plan had not, after all, been to go all the way to Panama but rather to retrace our steps, it seemed that this was our chance, as Kelly had warned the group that unaccompanied migrants were strictly forbidden in this stretch of territory. Given my extensive experience in being neurotic, it was not difficult to summon a breakdown, and with the *albergue* man looming over me I begged Kelly to please take me back with her because I had changed my mind; I was too scared to go to America and would instead go live happily ever after in Medellín.

The man was not inclined to let me turn back, but Kelly, though also incredulous, won out. She became even more incredulous when Johan and Kelvin announced that they, too, had to turn back so as not to leave me alone, and over the four-hour return trek to where we had started she periodically reminded us of the quantity of money we had just lost, scolding Johan and Kelvin: "What were you thinking bringing this person into the jungle?" I was at least not bad at walking, she acknowledged, but that was about my only positive attribute, and she advised me to trust in God and recognize that fear and fatigue were all in my mind.

Kelly had two children, ages four and nine, and was training to be a nurse, but the trafficking gig helped pay the bills in the meantime. As in the Indigenous village of Bajo Chiquito in the Panamanian Darién, it's not difficult to comprehend the economic motives driving employment in the flourishing industry; it so happens that the largely Afro-Colombian department of Chocó, which includes Capurganá, is consistently the country's poorest, with poverty levels at times approaching 70 percent. That said, it's not like Kelly was rolling in dough as a guide. For nine hours of walking today, for example, she was earning 200,000

Colombian pesos, or approximately fifty dollars at the time—and yet the 200,000-peso days were few and far between. Kelly had moved her family to Medellín for a spell, where they had resided in none other than the Barrio Pablo Escobar, founded in the 1980s by—who else?—Pablo Escobar. She had quickly decided, however, that she was not a fan of city life, for reasons including that in the city "they kidnap you and sell your organs." The organ stuff appeared to constitute a particular preoccupation of Kelly's, and she declared that while she herself barely made ends meet financially, she would never accept money to kill someone for their organs.

Contending that as a guide she was providing a necessary service, Kelly nonetheless stated openly that "what we are doing is illegal"—the "we" presumably being some iteration of the Clan del Golfo-New Light nexus. If it was up to her, Kelly said, no one would have to pay to migrate "because who knows when we ourselves will have to migrate?" And while "we are seen as criminals," she said, she personally chose to see her work as offering protection to vulnerable people who would migrate regardless of the risks. As per Kelly's calculations, there were "no more *muertos* or rapes" in the selva, at least on the Colombian side, as the higher-ups in the "we" had enacted a violent crackdown on rapists and thieves in the interest of security; if you raped a migrant, in other words, you might very well end up dead. The yellow frog bracelets that had been affixed to our wrists were also for "security," she stated, although no further information was divulged on this subject. And on that note I'll go ahead and insert another reminder that while the United States prefers to blame the current "migration crisis" on the Kellys of the world, a much greater criminality lies in U.S. foreign policy and America's criminalization of migration, without which organized crime would be up a creek.

Kelly's brother worked the Carreto route, she told us, and could arrange passage for $500—less than the $750 paid by the Afghan migrants I had spoken with in Tapachula. This was a riskier route for the "we," though, and could result in eight years in prison if you were caught, a fate that had befallen two friends of hers. Among the guides working the land route from Capurganá and Acandí, the rationale for not escorting migrants all the way across the border was that they could then be arrested in Panama for international migrant trafficking, but it seemed like a good enough excuse to ditch people without having to walk so far, too. Kelly found the walking therapeutic, she told us, as it cleared her head of responsibilities at home, and she generally wasn't afraid to undertake the four-hour return trip to Capurganá by herself, only occasionally getting nervous when it got dark. Johan politely reminded her that fear was in her mind.

On the walk back we encountered an eighty-one-year-old Colombian man on a horse who stopped to tell us his age and all about his farm, which was located in the vicinity and boasted plentiful avocado trees, among other vegetation. He also broadcast that he was in the market for a wife, but a wife of around sixty years of age. He dismissed Kelly as far too young, despite her teasing offers to undergo all the operations necessary to achieve the perfect body, after which they could share the profits from the farm. The man would have been content to remain chatting until the end of time, but we had to keep moving and found ourselves once again at the mountain of mud, which now had to be navigated in the upward direction. Halfway up we came upon a seemingly Venezuelan family with their guide, the parents sitting in the mud discarding items from their multiple bags and debating whose fault it was that they had brought so many clothes. Detecting an opportunity, Kelly approached the family to see if they had anything that might fit her kids; she returned with a few garments, one of which she would subsequently leave on the path "for someone else."

At the top of the hill we found a group of some thirty people preparing to descend with their guide in what would soon be darkness. Howler monkeys had commenced making a racket from the trees, which pleased Kelvin, who had been counting on more interactions with wildlife despite Kelly's warning that "the monkeys shit on you and throw fruit." When we reached the relatively new plowed stretch of road, Kelly pledged that the "we" would continue to improve the thoroughfare, thus ensuring that there would be no shortage of complaints from those perturbed that the "*Tapón del Darién*"—the "Darién Plug," as it's rendered in Spanish—was no longer a "plug." There's also, of course, the matter of environmental damage and "vital rainforest" preservation that the United States likes to invoke as proof of the need to combat migration through the Darién Gap, as though the country whose military was ranked as "one of the largest climate polluters in history" in a 2019 Lancaster University study has any right to preach about saving the trees. According to Oxford University's Neta Crawford, author of *The Pentagon, Climate Change, and War: Charting the Rise and Fall of U.S. Military Emissions*, the U.S. Department of Defense is the single largest institutional emitter of greenhouse gases on the planet. This is no doubt crucial information to keep in mind when considering how many refugees said super-polluter has generated of its own accord in places like Afghanistan, some of whom then turn up on the other side of the world in the "vital rainforest." The arrangement merits further consideration still given the soaring number of "climate refugees"; as per a 2023 briefing by the European Parliament, more than 376 million people had been displaced since 2008 by climate disasters, the equivalent of one person per second, and in 2022 alone "36.2 million people were displaced because of natural disasters brought about by climate change."[79] The Institute for Economics and Peace, a global think tank headquartered in Sydney, Australia, has warned that, by 2050, some 1.2 billion people could be displaced by the climate crisis.[80]

The Darién Gap encompasses two UNESCO World Heritage Sites: the 72,000-hectare Los Katíos National Park on the Colombian side and its much larger counterpart, the Darién National Park of Panama, measuring 575,000 hectares. As the Washington, D.C.-based Center for Strategic and International Studies would put it in a May 2024 report titled *Mind the Darién Gap, Migration Bottleneck of the Americas*, the current mass movement through the

Gap was "creating an environmental disaster in one of the largest expanses of intact rainforest in the world [and] causing potentially irrevocable damage to the Western Hemisphere's 'most important "natural lung" after the Amazon.'" Not even the *muertos*, it seemed, had any respect for the environment, and the report lamented that "the scale of pollution is extreme: on top of corpses and bodily waste, the jungle is now littered with plastic bottles, empty food tins, and dirty diapers."

But dirty diapers ain't got nothing on the Pentagon—or on the industrial and corporate pollution that is regarded as entirely acceptable in capitalism even though it is literally annihilating the environment while the bodily waste of poor people is not. In April 2024, *The New York Times* observed that top Panamanian officials had taken to voicing "growing frustration with the financial and environmental cost that migration has inflicted on the small nation," as though Panama wasn't making bank busing migrants to Costa Rica and as though the government had not long kissed the ass of international corporations engaged in environmentally pernicious activities on Panamanian soil.[81] Over on the Colombian side of the Darién Gap, environmental preservation is such a risky undertaking that Colombia was pronounced the world's most dangerous country for environmentalists in 2022—a situation that hasn't exactly kept the political elite or the United States up at night. In her 1994 book *The Phantom Gringo Boat: Shamanic Discourse and Development in Panama*, Stephanie Kane offered what she admitted were probably some "overly romantic" musings on capitalist encroachment in the region: "If by some unlikely miracle the 'outside world' (e.g., loggers, miners, pesticide experts) can learn to forget this piece of forest, leaving a small gap in the destruction, the [Indigenous] Emberá of Darién may survive a good deal longer than the rest of humankind."[82] Three decades later, the Darién Gap hardly constitutes a "gap in the destruction," as it were—just look at all the dirty diapers!— but the damage is ultimately of a more symbolic nature. The Darién Gap, you might say, is emblematic of no less than the destruction of "humankind" by a global capitalist system that denies poor people dignity in life and death alike.

As Kelly, Johan, Kelvin, and I neared Capurganá, which was still without electricity, two men emerged from the darkness and fell into step beside us. One was the guide from the morning who had called me "Palestina" and who now addressed me with a sarcastic chuckle and a tone that caused even Johan to momentarily adopt a deer-in-headlights look: "So you're the one that felt bad and had to turn back?" I was saved by Kelly, who vouched for my utter uselessness in terms of fortitude and fibbed to her colleague that she would be putting me up in her house prior to returning me to Medellín whence I had come. This hypothetical arrangement proved acceptable and the men veered off, leaving us to catch an auto rickshaw to the *albergue*, where one final registration of the returned migrants was in order, and Kelly bid us farewell after giving Johan and Kelvin her number in case they wanted to face the jungle once more without me.

By this time all the walking had taken its toll, and we hobbled to the hotel to collect my passport and other belongings; aching legs would soon be added to the list of definitive nonproblems when we made the acquaintance of a Colombian man with an amputated foot who was collecting money from tourists in Capurganá to fund his own Darién Gap passage. There was no vacancy at the hotel that night, as the establishment had been taken over by a group of Europeans who had been boated in from Panama and were dancing on the deck, music and lights courtesy of the hotel's generator. We landed some bunk beds in an unventilated room down the street, and Kelvin and I awoke the next morning to find that Johan had migrated overnight to the floor between the bunks in search of salvation from the heat. Over the ensuing days we sluggishly made our way to Necoclí and then Medellín, where following a weepy hug Kelvin was put on a bus back to Cúcuta and his father's house. Johan would stay with me for another week before joining him.

Kelvin and I remained in touch, and later in the year I would send his mother Nelvis and six-year-old sister Tiffany—whom he hadn't seen in nearly four years—on their own bus odyssey from Caracas to Cúcuta to surprise him. In this case, the lack of travel documents for mother and sister was entirely irrelevant as the Venezuelan-Colombian border has never quite lived up to its name; when Amelia and I hitchhiked across said border in 2009, for example, we searched on both sides for someone to stamp our passports to no avail. For the surprise, I told Kelvin I needed him to go fetch a gringo journalist from the Cúcuta bus terminal and sent him a picture of *New York Times* foreign affairs columnist Thomas Friedman, thanks to whom I had lost a year of my life on a book dissecting the numerous highly remunerated theories to have sprung from his brain. These included that McDonald's was the key to world peace, that Afghanistan was a "special needs baby," that Iraqis needed to "Suck. On. This" as punishment for 9/11—an event Friedman himself admitted Iraq had nothing to do with—and that it was "not pretty, but it was logical" when Israel killed Arab civilians.[83] Over the course of his never-ending career Friedman had also managed a smattering of ruminations on Colombia, such as that time in 2010 when he hailed the country as "one of the great democratic success stories."[84] This assessment, mind you, came against the backdrop of not only the "false positives" scandal but also the so-called parapolitics scandal implicating a good chunk of the Colombian political class in paramilitary collaboration—but, hey, "democracy" is whatever empire says it is. Kelvin was not familiar with the Friedmanian oeuvre but was thrilled, needless to say, to find Nelvis and Tiffany at the bus terminal instead.

From Medellín Johan and I flew to the Colombian island of San Andrés, located closer to Nicaragua than to Colombia and known for the otherworldly blues of its waters. Nowadays, it was becoming increasingly known as a migration hot spot, as well—or as "A Second Darién Gap," as BBC News Mundo headlined it in a December 2023 article. The "VIP route" from San Andrés to Nicaragua by boat, which enabled migrants to circumvent the actual Darién Gap, could be booked for between $1,500 and $5,000, according to the Colombian Attorney General's Office, and in the past two years alone 977 Nicaragua-bound migrants had been rescued off the coast of San Andrés. Disappearance was also a potential outcome of the supposed "VIP route," and BBC News Mundo reported that family members of the disappeared who had taken to social media to ask for help had "received phone calls to extort them and death threats for insisting that the search" for the missing continue. Some family members had noted that the social media accounts of their loved ones had remained active following their disappearance.

In 2022, the Colombian media alliance La Liga Contra El Silencio (The League Against Silence) described San Andrés as "a paradise under the violent control of the Clan del Golfo"—although apparently not fully, as a "war for control of narcotrafficking routes" had since 2010 left 285 people dead and 700 disappeared, according to unofficial data. For its part, the Clan del Golfo was said to dominate the transport of cocaine that passed through San Andrés, operating via local criminal groups. And while the island was forever cast as a "dream destination" for rest and diversion, La Liga Contra El Silencio emphasized, this narrative concealed facts on the ground. In 2018, the homicide rate in San Andrés was 35.71 per 100,000 inhabitants, the highest in the Caribbean region; in 2020, in the midst of the coronavirus pandemic, it soared to 59.6, compared to 22.48 nationwide.[85] And as with the Darién Gap, drug smuggling routes now overlapped with migrant smuggling routes. In July 2024, Colombian media would report that a key migrant route out of San Andrés had come to be dominated by Tren de Aragua, the Venezuelan criminal outfit that concerned U.S. politicians have sought to portray as the latest existential threat to the homeland. In June, Florida senator Marco Rubio, the xenophobic son of Cuban immigrants, had taken to X to warn that "Tren de Aragua is causing terror across America as a result of President Biden's open border policy."[86]

When Johan and I landed at the diminutive San Andrés airport on January 22, he was immediately selected out of all of the arriving passengers to be hauled off to a special room and put through a drug-detecting machine. The Colombian anti-narcotics official amusedly granted my request to attend the inspection and pronounced Johan clean, leaving us free to exit the airport for five romantic days of intermittent sun and mind-altering winds, one of which we spent not speaking to each other on account of a disagreement over whether margarine counted as butter. In the car on the way from the airport to our accommodations, our Colombian host gave us a vague rundown on recent island happenings: a young man had died, and then at his funeral an older woman had died. We sought additional clarification, and our host expanded his explanation slightly to specify that the young man had died after being hit with a bullet and the woman had died when his funeral was shot up. I searched in vain for news of the killings online and only found them reported, several days later, in a weekly local paper that was sold at the supermarket. The killings had not been resolved, but the San Andrés police had triumphantly captured someone engaged in illegal fishing.

Johan and I rented a golf cart–type vehicle and made rounds of the island, stopping in at seaside shacks that served rum by the plastic cupful. At one such establishment we talked late into the night with the proprietors, a husband and wife, who complained about the *vacuna*—literally "vaccine"—that they were required to pay an unspecified armed group in order to operate in peace. The wife was plotting to take the couple's small son to the United States, she said, as she was certain she could finagle passage to Nicaragua from San Andrés at a discounted price. At another establishment we fell into conversation with an Afro-Colombian man whose first and middle names were Jimmy Carter. His grandfather, he told us, had served the U.S. military in the Panama Canal Zone, while he himself was involved in migrant transport; if Johan happened to be interested, the trip to Nicaragua was about six hours, although the boats weren't sailing at the moment on account of the wind—which is why Jimmy Carter was sitting on a rock drinking rum.

For the duration of the margarine altercation, meanwhile, I spent the day on the beach, where I made the acquaintance of a Paraguayan businessman from Asunción who was also avoiding his travel companion—a German businessman who according to my interlocutor had immigrated to Paraguay based on the country's lax drunk driving laws. The former friends had booked rooms at an all-inclusive hotel for their joint holiday on San Andrés, but the Paraguayan was now laying low outside the resort in the hopes that he wouldn't be found by the German, who, he said, had decided that being pro-Nazi was good for business. Not, of course, that Nazism was so foreign to the Southern Cone; just recall that time that Klaus Barbie, the World War II Gestapo chief known as the "Butcher of Lyon," was put on the postwar anti-communist payroll of U.S. intelligence and shipped off to South America. There, his exploits included participation in Operation Condor, a collaborative U.S.-backed effort among regional governments that was launched in 1975 and that saw tens of thousands of suspected leftists tortured, dropped from aircraft into bodies of water, and otherwise eliminated. In their book *Whiteout: The CIA, Drugs and the Press*, Alexander Cockburn and Jeffrey St. Clair document how Barbie went on to help "orchestrate the so-called 'cocaine coup' of 1980, when a junta of Bolivian generals seized power, slaughtering their leftist opponents and reaping billions in the cocaine boom."[87] Anyway, he was a hell of an anti-communist.

Our San Andrés "holiday" came to an end, and back Johan and I flew to Medellín, where Johan boarded his return bus to Cúcuta to spend the next month with his father and Kelvin prior to embarking on his third Darién Gap tour. We parted ways on the street, Johan proclaiming that notwithstanding our differences of opinion he still loved me and would see me soon, God willing, in

Washington. Unbeknownst to us at the time, he would see me even sooner in Mexico, but for now he was gone, taking with him the stuffed panda I had brought him from the Washington zoo, the duty-free cologne we had acquired in the San Andrés airport, and my dad's old sweatpants, all of which would accompany him into the jungle in March. Before leaving Medellín myself I chatted with an upper-middle-class septuagenarian resident of a neighborhood I had patronized purely for its name—Belén—and who had previously resided for twenty years in Connecticut. Two decades were sufficient, he said, to conclude that it was preferable to live in Colombia, a preference he acknowledged was not so easily exercised by Colombians lacking his financial security. He had tried to educate his rich friends as to the perils of unbridled capitalism and to persuade them that they perhaps did not need to be quite so rich; inequality, after all, was at the heart of Colombia's forever war: "Nobody goes and becomes a guerilla living under a bush in the selva for no reason." Just like nobody walks through the selva for a week if they don't have to.

From Medellín I flew to Panama and then on to Mexico, covering in a matter of hours a distance it would soon take Johan weeks to travel. In Mexico City I spent the night of February 2 near the airport in preparation for the final stretch "home" to Zipolite, and it was there, just after I had checked into my room, that I received a call from Yurbis in Chicago, who was screaming on the other end of the line. The screams gradually coalesced into the words "they killed her," and I learned through anguished sobs that Yurbis's eighteen-year-old niece Francis, the beloved daughter of Isamar, had been murdered by her Colombian boyfriend, who had then killed himself. Months earlier when the family had arrived at the decision to undertake the journey to the United States, Isamar had insisted that Francis stay behind with her grandmother in Venezuela, petrified as she was for her daughter's safety. Francis had then returned to the Colombian department of Nariño near the Ecuadorian border where she had lived with her mom and siblings for a time. And now she was dead.

I had not seen any *muertos* in the Darién Gap, thus undoubtedly failing to live up to Ryszard Kapuściński's dictum that "it's wrong to write about people without living through at least a little of what they are living through." But I now found myself confronted with a photograph, forwarded to me by Yurbis, of the bloated corpses of Francis and her boyfriend on the cracked and faded tiles of a kitchen floor in Nariño, with streams of coagulated blood emanating from their bodies and a gas stove and large cement sink in the background. The boyfriend lay face down and perpendicular to Francis, his feet centimeters from her head; she was face up in a yellow tank top and black shorts, her arms outstretched. In the foreground was an empty dog bowl. As I had corresponded with Francis on Facebook in December when I was freaking out about her family being incommunicado aboard La Bestia, I pulled up her Facebook page for the morbid social media examination that inevitably attends death these days. Just days prior to being killed, Francis had tagged her boyfriend in a post about wanting cute cow slippers, to which he had promised: "Tomorrow, amor." And on January 10, shortly after her family had arrived in the United States, she had tagged Isamar in a Spanish meme on people who "go to the USA and then start posting I miss my country." Then came the meme's climax: "If you want I'll call the *migra*."

Upon receiving the news about Francis, Isamar had locked herself in a room and refused to speak to anyone. Yurbis kept me apprised of Francis's posthumous migration back to Venezuela, her body transported by her grandfather—Isamar and Yurbis's dad—who had to raise money among his neighbors in order to fund the torturous journey to Nariño and back. By the time Francis's corpse made it home, she was in such bad shape that the wake and funeral had to be closed casket. Isamar would never forgive herself for trying to protect Francis by leaving her behind, and once she emerged from the locked room and resumed responding to messages, she wrote me: "They took my life away."

The American dream having thus been swiftly converted into an unmitigated nightmare, Isamar was left to be tormented by the realization that she had survived a deadly odyssey only to die on the inside, her daughter's death perceived as a direct consequence of her own migration. And while the Darién Gap with its countless unnamed, unburied *muertos* will continue to be notorious for all the things that can kill you within a 106-kilometer stretch of "green hell," the jungle is also much bigger than itself. Indeed, the Darién Gap encapsulates the inherent deadliness of borders—and, frequently, of life in general—for the have-nots of this earth, where imperial machinations and the tyranny of an elite minority help ensure that there will never be a shortage of folks who see no choice but to get up and start walking.

At the end of the day, the jungle is a microcosm of inequality in which the poor have to risk their lives to live—and are criminalized for doing so. And in that sense, then, the Darién Gap is the world.

On the morning of March 2, 2024, Johan entered the jungle from Acandí, his third trip into the Darién Gap in just over a year. I would have no news from him until the evening of March 5, two days before my forty-second birthday, and as I lay in my Zipolite hammock alternately wanting to die and grabbing the phone to see if the single WhatsApp check mark had turned into two, I made many promises to the universe. I would stop drinking, I would never again have fights over margarine, I would be more gracious, I would clean my house. I binge-scrolled through Face-book pages with names like "Perdidos en la selva del Darién" ("Lost in the Darién Jungle"), where people pleaded for informa-tion on missing loved ones and where total strangers comforted each other virtually, often prescribing faith in God. And I thought about a silver-haired man named Abed whom I had met during one of my stays in south Lebanon and whose brother Ahmad had been missing since 1983—one of an estimated seventeen thousand disappeared persons during the Lebanese civil war of 1975–90. Like so many other families, Abed's had been deprived of the emotional closure that would have been possible had they known Ahmad's fate; unable to even commence the grieving process without something concrete to grieve, they had instead spent the past several decades in a state of perpetual anguish and psycho-logical limbo. I spent three and a half days in anguish, and that was certainly enough.

Johan had arrived in Necoclí on February 26 but had been unable to depart for the jungle until March 2, as the boat companies operating out of Necoclí and Turbo had suspended their services following the arrest of two boat captains for transporting migrants. The Darién Gap had thus effectively been temporarily shut down, which while no doubt the wet dream of many a U.S. politician, was not exactly sustainable given the large numbers of migrants arriving daily at the Colombian coast. The Colombian government intervened and services resumed—only now passengers were required to purchase a *permiso* to travel from Migración Colombia, the Colombian immigration agency. Johan sent me a photo of his *permiso*, which included a picture of him looking utterly pissed off and which listed his birthdate, passport issue date, and passport expiration date all as January 1, 2000. In other words, business continued as usual but with Migración Colombia directly signing off on it and getting their own small piece of the pie with the *permisos*. The price of passage had also gone up since our visit in January, and this time around Johan paid $380 to a guide in Necoclí for the boat and trans-Darién trajectory. His group, which comprised Venezuelans and a handful of Syrians, was scheduled to depart on March 1, but excessive congestion at the port delayed them an additional day. Johan's last message to me before taking off was: "Me piensas un poquito"—"Think about me a little."

At 6.32 P.M. on March 5, the single check mark turned into two and there was Johan: "Mi amor bello I'm alive, I came out of the jungle this morning gracias a Dios. I'm super destroyed. But I'm alive." He was in Bajo Chiquito, where we had met almost exactly one year earlier, and informed me that he had thought of me the whole time in the jungle because it gave him "more strength"— which was enough to make me cry before he even told me the rest of the story. The journey from Acandí had been a far uglier experience this year, he said, with a lot more *muertos* than he had seen with Andrés, Felipe, and El Mono. Crossing into Panama, his group had been held up by armed men who had beaten him when he resisted handing over his money and had searched him from head to toe, making off with nearly $500 and leaving him with only a few small bills that were particularly well hidden. Some of the women in his group, he said, had been raped when they hadn't been able to produce any cash. The following month, *The New York Times* would report that sexual violence against migrants on the Panamanian side of the Darién Gap had reached a "level rarely seen outside war."[88] But this, too, was war—and the United States the chief belligerent.

The next day Johan would use what remained of his money to pay for the piragua to "*la ONU*,"—that is, the Lajas Blancas migrant reception station—having confirmed that it was no longer possible to slip out of Bajo Chiquito on foot as he had done the previous year. At Lajas Blancas he would be reunited with his cousin Sthefanie, who went by the nickname Chachi and had caught the boat from Necoclí to Acandí prior to the short-lived "closure" of the Darién Gap. Neither cousin had known of the other's migration, and the overlap had only been discovered by Johan's mom; learning that Johan was on his way, Chachi had waited for him in Panama. A twenty-four-year-old lesbian, Chachi had lived for the past five years in Medellín, where she had worked, inter alia, at a fast-food restaurant specializing in *salchipapas*, a dish made with French fries and sausage. The cousins hadn't spoken in years, but at their reunion in Lajas Blancas it was quickly established that Chachi had been colleagues in Medellín with none other than Javier, one of the Venezuelan components of the *Siete Magníficos*—the true bizarreness of which coincidence it took all of us a while to wrap our heads around.

Chachi would later tell me that while Johan had been odious to her as a kid, he was now her "angel sent by God" to rescue her in Panama, where she had very nearly given up and gone back to Colombia. She had made the crossing from Acandí in three days, during which a knee injury had flared up and rendered walking so excruciating that she begged her group to abandon her in the forest. She had not been sexually assaulted, but she had witnessed other women be made to squat so as to facilitate the search for money potentially hidden in their intimate parts. At Lajas Blancas the cousins would see a young man begging for help to retrieve the corpse of his father from the jungle; Johan had passed the young man and not-yet-dead dad along the way and had noted that the son had appeared to be in denial: "You could tell the old guy wasn't going to make it, but the son was just like trying to believe he was just tired." From Lajas Blancas onward the cousins would travel as a pair, and Johan would develop a fierce loyalty to Chachi, who would never fail to coax him out of his bouts of crankiness and melancholy by jabbering loudly in made-up languages in public and choreographing TikTok routines featuring the two of them lip-synching to reggaetón.

After my mother in Washington had volunteered to do battle with Western Union in order to replenish Johan's cash supply, the cousins traversed Central America in record time. On March 13 they were shuttled from Guatemala City to the Guatemala-Mexico border by a friendly smuggler, who loaded them onto rafts to be deposited on the Mexican side of the river in the town of Ciudad Hidalgo, Chiapas, half an hour from Tapachula. And that's when stuff started to get complicated—first and foremost when they were detained for six scorching days and five sleepless nights in Ciudad Hidalgo, which had seemingly undergone spontaneous conversion into an open-air prison of sorts minus the complimentary food and water. Indeed, things had changed drastically in Chiapas just since my last visit four months earlier in November, when I had met Yurbis and Isamar; whereas refuge seekers arriving from Guatemala had previously been able to leave Ciudad Hidalgo with relative ease and continue on their way, Johan and Chachi were now informed that attempting to depart the town of their own accord would immediately deliver them into the hands of the cartels. Naturally, COMAR—the Mexican Commission for Refugee Assistance, where migrants could theoretically apply for protection in Mexico—had zero presence in Ciudad Hidalgo.

With elections rapidly approaching in the United States, Mexico was under increasing pressure to make life as miserable and obstacle-ridden as possible for U.S.-bound migrants, and Mexican President Andrés Manuel López Obrador (AMLO) faithfully carried out his work as U.S. gatekeeper and last line of defense even while continuing to fancy himself an anti-neoliberal hero who was forever sticking it to the gringos. Mexico, too, was gearing up for the country's largest-ever elections in June, which would also turn out to be the bloodiest in Mexican history, as criminal groups ramped up violence in the run-up to the electoral spectacle. I wouldn't fully comprehend the extent to which the border landscape had been altered until I asked various acquaintances in Tapachula if they wouldn't mind going to retrieve Johan and Chachi from Ciudad Hidalgo in exchange for payment and was politely turned down: "If we pick up migrants, the cartels will kill us." As in the Darién Gap, Mexican drug-trafficking organizations had taken control of migrant smuggling operations, as well—and they weren't keen to lose any customers.

The only ticket out of Ciudad Hidalgo, according to Johan, was on buses arranged by the Mexican immigration personnel who were overseeing the mass informal detention on the border. These buses were destined for the city of Arriaga in western Chiapas, the migrants were told, and the stated price fluctuated between free and one hundred dollars. Johan's and Chachi's names were added to the infinite list of passengers for the Arriaga bus, and they set about waiting with nothing to do aside from sit in the sun all day and reflect on their acute physical discomfort and deteriorating psychological state. I was still in Zipolite in the neighboring state of Oaxaca, and unable to stand the vicarious torment, I determined to do my part to aid and abet the migrant invasion of the United States by renting a car and driving to Chiapas for Johan and Chachi. I had no precise plan, but some significant movement was clearly needed in order to keep me from feeling inert and purposeless, and I figured that in the very least I could pick them up in

Arriaga and drive them as far as Oaxaca City 250 kilometers north of Zipolite, where it would be a straight shot on to Mexico City.

First, however, I had to contend with another first-world travel problem, which was that my valid U.S. driver's license was at my mother's apartment in Washington, D.C., and my mother was in Barcelona on her first trip back without my dad. My Mexican landlord offered to rent the car for me before discovering that his license was expired—at which point it suddenly occurred to me that my old Texas driver's license, which I did have in my possession in Zipolite, bore the expiration date 03/07/2024. In the United States this of course meant March 7, my birthday, but for once it seemed that America's insistence on doing everything backwards and confounding the rest of the world with its dates and measurements was going to work in my favor. Sure enough, the rental car company at the airport in nearby Huatulco interpreted the license expiration date as July 3, meaning I still had a good several months to go, and off I went to Chiapas, arriving some seven hours later in Arriaga on the afternoon of March 18. Tempted by the crates of mangoes lining the side of the road, I stopped to purchase one from an elderly woman who congratulated me on my unwed state because "men are nothing but trouble."

Johan and Chachi had been strung along all day with promises of the imminent departure of the Arriaga bus, and just as I arrived in the city Johan reported that they were at last in line to board the mythical vehicle. I booked a hotel room and set about eating mangoes, and a final message from Johan notified me that he would be out of touch for the duration of the ride as he was being made to store his phone in the baggage compartment below. Around midnight he reappeared online, and it was revealed that the Arriaga bus had not been bound for Arriaga at all but rather for the city of Tuxtla Gutiérrez, more than two hours to the northeast. It was agreed that I would sleep for a few hours and set out before sunrise to collect them.

I arrived in Tuxtla Gutiérrez to find that it was a rather more gigantic metropolis than I had thought, and incapable as ever of understanding driving directions on the phone, I tracked Johan and Chachi down thanks only to the benevolent intervention of another motorist, who told me to follow him across half the city. There, finally, in the parking lot of an Oxxo convenience store, were Johan, Chachi, and the stuffed panda from the Washington zoo, who had also survived the Darién Gap. There were cathartic hugs and big smiles all around, as even total exhaustion could apparently not dampen the cousins' elation at no longer being in Ciudad Hidalgo. They had two backpacks and another bag between them, and Johan was rocking his latest fashion statement—striped athletic shorts over black leggings—to which ensemble a balaclava would later be added. We piled into the car for the drive back to Arriaga, where I had booked another night at the hotel so that Johan and Chachi could shower, eat, rest, and perform other basic activities taken for granted by the privileged traveler. Seeing as Chachi had been without any semblance of privacy since leaving Medellín weeks before, I got her a separate hotel room, which she took full advantage of to produce new TikTok content. Johan fell asleep in my arms only to spend the rest of the night thrashing around, which according to Chachi was what had happened every time he had managed to sleep since exiting the jungle.

We departed Arriaga at 9 A.M. on March 20 in high spirits, our only worldly concern for the moment being how to program the stereo of the rental car to transmit the desired reggaetón playlist. I had gone ahead and reserved an apartment for us for that night in Oaxaca City, so entrenched was my conviction in my own inalienable freedom of movement that it never occurred to me we might not actually get there. But the reality check was swift, and we had advanced no more than a few kilometers from the hotel before we found ourselves in the midst of a checkpoint swarming with police officers and officials from the Chiapas attorney general's office. Rolling down the window while hissing at Johan out of the side of my mouth to try to look as gringo as possible, I asked for directions to the beach in what I thought was a most convincing clueless American tourist accent. Our friends were not so easily fooled, and once Johan and Chachi had identified their national origins, we were commanded to pull over and remove ourselves from the vehicle.

There commenced a thorough inspection of all of our possessions, including the inside of my wallet and our cell phones, despite Chachi's courteous observation that such behavior was not in fact legal. The sole female police officer among the swarm of characters, who was casually smoking a cigarette with a tattered face mask draped across her chin, gave us a "good cop" wink as the content of our communication devices underwent review on the side of the road: "Well, we all have naked pictures on our phones, don't we?" This same cop suggested repeatedly that I gift her my sunglasses, while I proceeded in pretending to only speak English, an act that had to be revised when the ringleader of the operation began broadcasting audio messages I had sent in Spanish for all to hear. Throughout all of this, migrants of varying nationalities streamed past the checkpoint on foot, and we were lectured by our antagonists that pedestrian movement by migrants was perfectly permissible and would not elicit intervention by the Mexican powers that be—a claim that would soon enough prove to be entirely false.

Prior to the confiscation of my phone I had managed to place a quick call to my friend in Zipolite who knew someone with connections to higher-ups in the *migra*; hitting redial, the police asked him to identify himself and were sadistically tickled when he said he was my boyfriend, the very role we had just told them was occupied by Johan. Wagering that they had really hit the jackpot here, a pair of police made off with my phone for further investigation while the others got down to business: I would need to produce 50,000 Mexican pesos (approximately $3,000) or they would impound the car, put me in jail for migrant trafficking, and send Johan and Chachi back to the Guatemalan border.

While this would no doubt have been an educational follow-up to my stint in the Siglo XXI migrant jail, it was not an experience I wanted to have; nor, however, did I have access to 50,000 pesos. I went about ingratiating myself with an obese official from the attorney general's office who was sitting godfather-style in a pickup truck and who assured me he was very moved by the plight of migrants in Mexico, and Johan and Chachi went about negotiating the bribe down to around $500, which was the lowest the police would go since the money had to be divided between so many of them. My phone was returned to my possession and the godfather shook my hand, instructing me to drive Johan and Chachi as far as the next gas station five minutes down the road and to drop them off there, such that they might join all the other refuge seekers walking happily to the United States in the blistering sun. Naturally, another checkpoint materialized before the gas station did, and I was once again alerted to the fact that I was committing a crime punishable with jail time by transporting "illegals." My patience having already been obliterated, I bellowed that I was following explicit orders from the last checkpoint, whose guardians had furthermore relieved me of $500, whereupon I was accused of fueling corruption in Mexico by having acceded to the demand for a bribe.

These officials emitted some half-hearted threats and one of them then asked for my phone, this time to indicate to Johan and Chachi the route they were to take to circumvent the next two checkpoints, the first belonging to the Mexican National Guard and the second to the National Migration Institute, or INM. The latter checkpoint was located just beyond the Chiapas-Oaxaca state border, and according to our spontaneously friendly self-appointed guide, I could pick my passengers up on the other side of the *migra*, after which it would be smooth sailing from there on out. This was not at all the case, and Johan and Chachi were promptly ambushed while skirting the first checkpoint by National Guard agents, who were lurking in the bushes and who appropriated their meager cash. AMLO's pride and joy, the National Guard was created in 2019 and in no time at all had racked up all manner of accusations of torture, forced disappearances, extrajudicial killings, and sexual violence against asylum seekers. In 2020, just a year after the institution's birth and shortly after the onset of the pandemic, Amnesty International described an incident at the Siglo XXI detention center in which some twenty National Guard members were deployed to deal with detainees who were—quite validly—protesting that their incarceration was conducive to the contraction of COVID-19: "Flanked by Mexican immigration agents, the National Guard allegedly assaulted the migrants over several hours, stripping some of them naked and attacking them with their shields, fists, boots, hoses, fire extinguishers, pepper spray, Tasers, bats and knuckledusters, according to transcripts of interviews that the Fray Matías de Córdova Human Rights Center conducted with witnesses and shared with Amnesty International."[89]

After being robbed by the National Guard, Johan and Chachi were detained by the INM, who ordered their phones turned off. Having driven ahead in the car, I was oblivious to all that had happened, knowing only that my WhatsApp messages to the cousins were not going through. I drove around in circles for a bit and decided I might as well start drinking beer in order to cope with the heat and uncertainty. Ten minutes into the beer program I of course had to pee and pulled into a gas station with a contingent from the National Guard parked out front. They stopped the car to ask where I was coming from ("Arriaga") and where I was heading ("the bathroom"), and although there were some comments made on the open beer in the cup holder and the three others waiting to go in the passenger's seat, drinking and driving was clearly a less serious infraction than giving Venezuelans a ride.

After hanging around the gas station parking lot for an hour or so, I drove the short distance back to Chiapas, bought more beer, turned around, and drove through the National Guard and INM checkpoints again, still with no sign of Johan and Chachi. I parked the car under a bridge just past the INM, where there were a couple of food stands and a bevy of taxis, which I would only learn much later in the day were dedicated to ferrying migrants, for a hefty fee, past the National Guard post at the gas station and on to the town of San Pedro Tapanatepec on the Isthmus of Tehuantepec.

Evidently cartel-coordinated, the taxi service thrived with the complicity of said National Guard itself. For the moment I didn't have much of an opportunity to observe my surroundings as a man strolled over, followed by several other men, to peer into the car and inquire as to the nature of my business under the bridge. I was just drinking beer and waiting for some friends, I said, as one does. Upon learning my nationality, the first man volunteered that he was from the state of Sinaloa but had been sentenced to fifteen years in prison in the United States in 2020 for trafficking migrants across the border; the pandemic had served as a get-out-of-jail-free card, however, and he had been deported to Mexico after only fifteen days. When I asked what he currently did to occupy his time, he glanced at one of the other men and replied with a smirk: "Let's say I work with livestock." When the men began suggesting that we take a ride in my car, I decided this was as good a time as any to thank them for their hospitality and get the fuck out of there.

At around 3 P.M., six hours after we had set out from the hotel in Arriaga, Johan and Chachi reappeared in unison online to advise me that they were on the side of the road in the city of Berriozábal, just outside Tuxtla Gutiérrez, where the *migra* had deposited them along with a bus full of other intercepted migrants. Back I sped to Berriozábal, and back we sped to Arriaga, arriving at 7 P.M. only to find ourselves smack at the morning's first checkpoint, manned by the very same cast of characters. Momentarily paralyzed with fear, the beer in me won out and I pulled over before being ordered to and descended from the car, slamming the door behind me. I trusted everyone remembered me, I said, and had gotten a kick out of sending us straight into the clutches of another checkpoint that morning. In light of the day's progress, I had decided to write an article about migrant extortion in Mexico; would anyone like to be quoted in it?

The police dealt with this announcement by shouting that the *migra* was coming and for us to scram, which we did. The next checkpoint had now been dismantled, but the National Guard and

INM checkpoints were still there, and Johan and Chachi had no choice but to once again attempt the pedestrian detour through the bushes, now in the dark. This time they made it, but only after explaining to the National Guard agents who had once again pounced that all of their money had already been taken during the previous assault. I picked them up under the same bridge where I had met the fellow from Sinaloa, which was much less populated than during the daytime and where a man approached the car as the cousins were getting in: "Where are you going?" I dismissed the question with a wave of my hand and an "I was here earlier in the day," as though this constituted a blanket justification, and peeled out onto the highway.

By this time it was clear that we were not making it to Oaxaca City that night, but convinced that the worst was now behind us, I figured we could at least get to Juchitán, the isthmian city where I had encountered the hotel full of Mauritanians. The first wrench was thrown in the works when the drivers of the migrant-shuttling taxis that were gathered under the bridge—who were apparently none too pleased at losing a pair of customers to a meddlesome gringa—phoned ahead to the National Guard at the gas station to notify them that a migrant-trafficking case was heading their way. This, at any rate, was what I gathered from the three members of the National Guard who came barreling down the road in their pickup truck and cornered us in the parking lot preceding the gas station where we had stopped to plot our next moves.

Descending from the truck, the officers berated Johan and Chachi for putting me in this position of criminality and announced that from my Mexican jail cell I would be a stain on the national pride of the United States. Unmoved by my rambling speech about how all of this was my own country's fault anyway, they set about suggesting that jail time could potentially be avoided were I to provide a bit of "soda money" and were not impressed when in my audacious naïveté I assumed they literally meant enough money for three soft drinks. One of the agents made me google myself on his phone so as to verify that I was actually a journalist, after which it was established that 2,000 Mexican pesos—approximately $100—would be sufficient for soda. Disgruntled to hear that all of my pesos had already been distributed to their fellow forces of law and order, the National Guard debated having me charge the payment to my credit card at the gas station and collecting the cash from the station attendant. The officers then received a call seemingly alerting them to a higher-value operation somewhere in the vicinity and remounted their pickup truck, leaving us with the warning that Johan and Chachi were not allowed back in the car.

On the far side of the parking lot was another group of migrants whom Chachi was dispatched to interrogate. She returned with an eighteen-year-old Venezuelan who had been stuck in Mexico for almost a year and had been returned three times to the Guatemalan border, once after having made it all the way to Ciudad Juárez on the Texas frontier. This young man knew all the checkpoints between here and Juchitán like the back of his hand and offered to act as guide in exchange for something to eat. The next few checkpoints were a rousing success, with the three Venezuelans clearing them on foot and me picking them up on the other side. Our downfall came in the town of Niltepec, an hour from Juchitán, where we thought things had also gone off without a hitch until we found ourselves being chased down by a car with flashing lights.

It was nearly one in the morning, and the car belonged to some branch of the Mexican security apparatus I had never even heard of. The officers were blunt with me: If I was caught engaging in criminal behavior one more time, I was going behind bars for sure, and my passport was photographed along with the car. For now, I was to continue driving straight, while Johan, Chachi, and the eighteen-year-old would be accompanying whatever branch of the Mexican security apparatus this was back to the Niltepec checkpoint. We hugged, Chachi cried, and the Venezuelans were gone, taking the reggaetón playlist with them. I drove on in a daze to the next town, which, as luck would have it, was Santo

Domingo Ingenio, the very town where I had met up with Yurbis and Isamar on Thanksgiving and where they had told me that they would take the Darién Gap over Mexico any day.

I slept the remainder of the night at a hotel in Santo Domingo Ingenio; Johan and Chachi slept outdoors on the ground in Niltepec, awaking before dawn to start walking. Around mid-morning I met them at the entrance to Santo Domingo Ingenio, where under the watchful eyes of the drivers of the myriad taxis, minibuses, and motor scooters assembled to cater to varying migrant budgets, we came to terms with the fact that our joint road trip was over. While there was nothing I hated more than conceding defeat to the system, I clearly was not making Johan's and Chachi's lives any easier by trying to give them a ride, as solidarity had effectively been criminalized in the interest of profit—the whole point of capitalism. From here on out I would limit myself to financial support for the cousins, which was not always helpful, either. When on March 22 I bought them bus tickets online to travel from Juchitán to Oaxaca City, they were removed from the bus at an INM checkpoint and sent back to Arriaga to cover the same ground yet again. This time, Chachi told me, Johan cried, too.

During my internment in Siglo XXI, one of the Cuban inmates had noted that at least in the Darién jungle you were focused on moving forward and didn't have much time to dwell on anything else—unlike in migrant jail, where the suspension of mobility allowed all the trauma of the journey to catch up to you. And while Johan and Chachi were obviously not locked up, there was still a carceral aspect to their inability to move forward of their own free will without being returned to where they started from. They eventually broke free of Chiapas, at least, and began advancing slowly toward Oaxaca City, which on March 26 brought them through the town of San Pedro Pochutla, 15 kilometers from my house in Zipolite. I met them in the parking lot of the Chedraui supermarket, where they recounted their latest adventures running from the *migra* in the middle of the night. They arrived at last in Mexico City, generally regarded as a safe zone for migrants, in the wee hours of the morning of March 30, which was seventeen days after they had crossed the river into Mexico from Guatemala. The same distance is covered in less than two hours on a commercial flight.

In the Mexican capital I booked them accommodations that did not entail sleeping on the floor in a room with a dozen other people and an outdoor toilet, the situation in which many of their acquaintances had found themselves in the city. And on April 3 I flew from Huatulco to Mexico City to pay them a visit in what would be their indefinite home, as they had committed to waiting for CBP One appointments to cross into the United States rather than just turning up in El Paso as Johan had done the previous year. These appointments could only be applied for via the CBP One app from northern and central Mexico, which meant that the United States was basically requiring refuge seekers to migrate "illegally"—with all of the attendant perils—in order to reach a specific geographical location where they were entitled to request legal entrance to the United States. In August 2024 the system would be amended to permit non-Mexican migrants to request CBP One appointments from Chiapas as well as the adjacent state of Tabasco, meaning that "migrants who cross Mexico's southern border can now wait in Southern Mexico to secure an appointment before traveling to the north," as the U.S. Customs and Border Protection website put it.[90]

On our first morning together in the eighth-largest city in the world, we were returning from an outing to the pharmacy in the Anzures neighborhood when whom should we run into but four Chinese migrants Johan and Chachi had met in Panama. Cries of joy ensued, and I was introduced to the Chinese, who consisted of a couple, their twelve-year-old daughter, and a family friend. As they spoke neither English nor Spanish, all communications were conducted through the translation app the Chinese had on their phones, which is how we learned they were staying in a hotel for approximately twenty-five dollars per night with a bunch of "Taliban." This would no doubt have been music to the ears of the anti-immigrant crowd in the United States had further investigation not revealed that the phone app had some glitches and that the other hotel guests were merely from Afghanistan. The "Taliban" had told the Chinese to beware of CBP One scams—a warning Johan, Chachi, and I would have done well to heed—and had been waiting in Mexico City for their own appointments for eight months.

The Chinese had signed up to cross the Darién Gap via Carreto, one of the more expensive routes advertised as safer, quicker, and less taxing. Other migrants I had spoken with who had gone through Carreto reported just a day of walking; the Chinese had walked for four but had still been charged $700 each. The guide who had accompanied them—and whom the phone translation app intriguingly rendered as the "internal medicine guide"—had been a "liar," the wife said, and she had given him shit for it with the help of the app. She had also forced him to put her daughter on a horse for part of the crossing, but on the bright side they had seen no dead people or rapes. The family was bound for California, the wife told me, because the education system in China was bad, the students were brainwashed, and there were old people living on the streets. In that respect, then, they just might feel right at home in the United States.

Johan and Chachi were scammed twice in the pursuit of CBP One appointments, the first time by a female INM officer who sent them a fake appointment confirmation and the second time by a friend of a friend who never sent them anything at all. In June they managed to apply on their own for the appointments using Johan's phone, once the system stopped crashing long enough to let them hit enter. They landed construction work in Mexico City, for which Johan was paid about $1.80 per hour for ten-hour workdays and Chachi was paid less. As Johan continuously stressed to me, he was under no illusions that the United States was some sort of paradise and was even fully prepared to accept my classification of my country as a "*país de mierda*." However, he still thought he should be allowed to see it for himself and to work his ass off to send a bit of money back to his family—which, at the end of the day, would be enough of an "American dream" for him. Six months passed with no news from CBP One, and Johan increasingly made his despair known. What happens to a dream deferred?

To be sure, there was no lack of work in America, as perhaps evidenced by the fact that the *Siete Magníficos* who had crossed successfully in 2023 were already making more money than I did. Furthermore, the very economy of the United States happens to be rather dependent on migrant labor. Recall the calculation by the U.S. Chamber of Commerce itself that "if every unemployed person in the country found a job, we would still have millions of open jobs." Or consider a May 2024 CNBC analysis according to which America's "strong jobs market has been bolstered postpandemic by strength in the immigrant workforce," with immigrant workers making up a record 18.6 percent of the workforce in 2023. The analysis continued: "And as Americans age out of the labor force and birth rates remain low, economists and the Federal Reserve are touting the importance of immigrant workers for overall future economic growth."[91]

And yet the demonization of migrants proceeds apace, serving as it does as a politically expedient means to distract attention from actual problems. These might include, say, that the U.S. government spent $916 billion on the military in 2023 alone, the same year that a University of California, Riverside, study found poverty to be the fourth-leading cause of death among Americans. From the perspective of capitalism, the advantage of making migration to the United States as hellish an undertaking as possible is that migrants who have been worn down physically and psychologically over a period of months or even years aren't liable to demand many rights, whether in or out of the workplace.

In Spanish, the Darién Gap is known as *el Tapón del Darién*, or "Darién Plug." As part of a short-lived attempt to have the "plug" live up to its name, incoming Panamanian president José Raúl Mulino pledged upon taking office in July 2024 to shut down the

Darién Gap with the help of U.S.-financed repatriation flights. More than 190,000 people had thus far crossed the Gap that year, with at least 4,499 people—among them 901 minors—reportedly arriving in just the first six days in June. In his July 1 inauguration speech, Mulino stated: "I understand that there are profound reasons for migration, but each country needs to resolve its own problems."[92] And what do you know: Just a few weeks later he was quoted by the Associated Press as having determined that "this is a United States problem that we are managing"—and that any U.S.-funded repatriation from Panama would be voluntary.[93] In other words, the Darién Plug remained open for business.

For its part, Mexico is more of a plug than ever—a Siglo XXI writ large, if you will—where the "United States problem" has also produced all manner of business opportunities in denying people the freedom of movement and otherwise monetizing the suffering of a captive migrant population. Meanwhile, the unilateral sacrosanctity of the U.S. border holds firm, with the fallout felt across the world, from the Darién Gap to Haiti to Afghanistan and beyond. In terms of trafficking in human misery, the land of liberty knows no bounds.

Notes

Introduction

1. Although "Darién Gap" and "Darién jungle" do not denote the exact same geographic space—as not all of the Gap is considered jungle—the terms are often used interchangeably.
2. Facing History and Ourselves, *Eyes on the Prize: America's Civil Rights Movement, 1954–1985; A Study Guide to the Television Series* (Blackside, Inc., 2006), 154.
3. Uriel J. García, "Abbott's Immigration Rhetoric Criticized Again after Interview Response about Shooting Migrants," *The Texas Tribune*, Jan. 11, 2024.

The Darién Gap

1. Eduardo Galeano, *Genesis: Memory of Fire, Volume 1* (Nation Books, 2010), 58–59.
2. Franz Lidz, "Following in the Footsteps of Balboa," *Smithsonian Magazine*, Sept. 2013.
3. Robert C. Schwaller, *African Maroons in Sixteenth-Century Panama: A History in Documents* (Oxford University Press, 2021), 15–16.
4. Hunter Walker, "House GOPers Teamed with Conspiracist Who Called Migrants 'Apes' and 'Congo Cannibals,'" *Talking Points Memo*, Mar. 15, 2024.
5. See Laura Loomer (@LauraLoomer), "Exclusive video: Late last night in Darién Gap Panama," X, Feb. 20, 2024, https://x.com/LauraLoomer

/status/1760126727366586582; "Exclusive video from Panama jungle migrant camp: Group of Afghani Muslim men," X, Feb. 21, 2024, https://x.com/LauraLoomer/status/1760126727366586582; "Watch: Chinese invader in Darien Gap," X, Feb. 22, 2024, https://x.com /LauraLoomer/status/1760717209158971413; and "Must watch exclusive video: Venezuelans invaders, " X, Feb. 23, 2024, https://x.com /LauraLoomer/status/1761115606034546842.

6. Andy Newman, Julie Turkewitz, and Juan Arredondo, "Adams Went South to Deter Migrants: Many Say They'll Come Anyway," *The New York Times*, Oct. 7, 2023.

7. Cindy Carcamo and Andrea Castillo, "'Do Not Come': Kamala Harris' Three Words to Guatemalans Stir Debate and Backlash," *Los Angeles Times*, June 9, 2021.

8. William Paterson, "A Proposal to Plant a Colony in Darien; to Protect the Indians against Spain; and to Open the Trade of South America to All Nations," in *The Writings of William Paterson*, ed. S. Burton (Effingham Wilson, 1858), vol. 1, 159.

9. Martin Mitchinson, *The Darien Gap: Travels in the Rainforest of Panama* (Harbour Publishing, 2008), 199–200.

10. Craig Williams, "The Darien Scheme: How Scotland's Colonial Disaster Lives On," *The Herald*, Aug. 4, 2023.

11. David McCullough, *The Path Between the Seas: The Creation of the Panama Canal 1870–1914* (Simon & Schuster, 1978), 250.

12. Todd Balf, *The Darkest Jungle: The True Story of the Darién Expedition and America's Ill-Fated Race to Connect the Seas* (Crown, 2003), 303.

13. Balf, *Darkest Jungle*, 145.

14. Balf, *Darkest Jungle*, 169.

15. Balf, *Darkest Jungle*, 153.

16. "Celebrating in Style," *Land Rover Monthly*, Apr. 15, 2023.

17. McCullough, *Path Between the Seas*, 379.

18. McCullough, *Path Between the Seas*, 379.

19. Colombia is divided into thirty-two departments or administrative divisions plus the capital district of Bogotá.

20. Stephanie Kane, *The Phantom Gringo Boat: Shamanic Discourse and Development in Panama* (Smithsonian Institution Press, 1994), 72.

21. Kane, *Phantom Gringo Boat*, 126–128.

22. Juan Gossaín, "Procedente del latín, es el vocablo al que más se recurre para designar algo cuyo nombre se ignora," *El Tiempo*, Aug. 13, 2015 (translation mine).

23. See Curt Mills, "'We Think The Price Is Worth It,' Madeleine Albright: 1937–2022," *The American Conservative*, Mar. 25, 2022.

24. Gary Cohn and Ginger Thompson, "Torturers' Confessions: Now in Exile, These CIA-Trained Hondurans Describe Their Lives—And the Deaths of Their Victims," *The Baltimore Sun*, June 13, 1995.

25. "OOPS!: Noriega 'Cocaine' Was Tamales," *Los Angeles Times*, Jan. 23, 1990.

26. Physicians for Human Rights, "Operation 'Just Cause': The Human Cost of Military Action in Panama," October 1991, p. 15, https://phr .org/wp-content/uploads/1991/10/Operation-Just-Cause-The-Human -Cost-of-Military-Action-in-Panama.pdf.

27. David Adams, "An Overlooked Hero and the Forgotten Victims," *Tampa Bay Times*, Dec. 20, 1999.

28. Inter-American Commission on Human Rights, Annual Report 2022: Follow-up Factsheet of Report No. 121/18, Case 10.573 José Isabel Salas Galindo et. al. (United States), https://www.oas.org/en/IACHR/docs /annual/2022/docs/IA2022cap.2.g.US10.573-en.docx.

29. John Weeks and Phil Gunson, *Panama: Made in the USA* (Latin America Bureau, 1990), 110.

30. Quoted in McCullough, *Path Between the Seas*, 331.

31. McCullough, *Path Between the Seas*, 329.

32. McCullough, *Path Between the Seas*, 575.

33. Noam Chomsky, *What Uncle Sam Really Wants* (Odonian Press, 1993), 56.

34. Aggelos Petropoulos and Richard Engel, "A Panama Tower Carries Trump's Name and Ties to Organized Crime," NBC News, Nov. 17, 2017.

35. "Darien Jungle in 4 Days—Explore the Magical Rainforest," Tao Travel 365, accessed Nov. 9, 2024, https://taotravel365.tours/tour/darien -jungle-four-days/.

36. Erica Trujillo R., "Terrorífico. Cadáver fue hallado en un camión de basura," *El Siglo*, Feb. 2, 2023.

37. "China Blasts US over 'Hysterical' Balloon Claim," *Al Jazeera*, Feb. 18, 2023.

38. Catalina Oquendo, "Un informe de la ONU denuncia que autoridades de Panamá abusaron sexualmente de migrantes que cruzaron el Darién," *El País*, Feb. 11, 2023.

39. "Panamá rechaza señalamientos por supuestas violaciones a migrantes en Darién," *TVN Panamá*, Feb. 11, 2023.

40. "U.S., Colombian and Panamanian Officials Visit Darien Gap to Strengthen Migration Cooperation," U.S. Embassy Bogotá, Feb. 16, 2023.

41. "DHS and DOJ Propose Rule to Incentivize Lawful Migration Processes," U.S. Department of Homeland Security, Feb. 21, 2023.

42. Todd Miller, *Empire of Borders: The Expansion of the U.S. Border around the World* (Verso, 2019), 184.

43. Miller, *Empire of Borders*, 11.

44. Miller, *Empire of Borders*, 2.

45. "CBP Designs CBP One™ Mobile App to Streamline Lawful Travel to United States," U.S. Customs and Border Protection, Feb. 22, 2021, https://www.cbp.gov/newsroom/national-media-release/cbp-designs -cbp-one-mobile-app-streamline-lawful-travel-united.

46. "CBP One™ Mobile Application," U.S. Customs and Border Protection official website, accessed Nov. 9 2024, https://www.cbp.gov/about /mobile-apps-directory/cbpone.

47. John Washington, "Glitchy CBP One App Turning Volunteers Into Geek Squad Support for Asylum-Seekers in Nogales," *AZ Luminaria*, Mar. 20, 2023.

48. Grisel Bethancourt, "Bajo Chiquito: El pueblo selvático que la migración transformó," *La Prensa*, June 27, 2023.

49. Kane, *Phantom Gringo Boat*, 1–2.

50. Harsha Walia, *Border and Rule: Global Migration, Capitalism, and the Rise of Racist Nationalism* (Haymarket Books, 2021), 16.

51. Walia, *Border and Rule*, 14.

52. Jarrett Renshaw, "Biden Says U.S. Will Withhold Weapons from Israel if it Invades Rafah," Reuters, May 9, 2024.

53. Joan Didion, *Slouching Towards Bethlehem* (Farrar, Straus and Giroux, 1968), xvi.

54. James C. McKinley Jr., "Homeless Haitians Told Not to Flee to U.S.," *The New York Times*, Jan. 18, 2010.

55. "Former U.S. Diplomat Abrams to Lead Efforts on Venezuela," Reuters, Jan. 25, 2019.

56. See Michael Galant, "Trump's Sanctions Are Still Hurting Everyday Venezuelans—and Fueling Migration," *The Hill*, Jan. 27, 2024.

57. See Aline Barros, "U.S. Government to Resume Deportations to Venezuela," *Voice of America English News*, Oct. 5, 2023.

58. Donald Trump (@realDonaldTrump), X, Oct. 22, 2018, https://x.com/realDonaldTrump/status/1054351078328885248.

59. Stephanie Ferguson Melhorn, "Understanding America's Labor Shortage," U.S. Chamber of Commerce, Oct. 15, 2024, https://www.uschamber.com/workforce/understanding-americas-labor-shortage.

60. Oliver Villar and Drew Cottle, *Cocaine, Death Squads, and the War on Terror: U.S. Imperialism and Class Struggle in Colombia* (Monthly Review Press, 2011), 54.

61. Secretary Colin L. Powell, "Designation of the AUC As a Foreign Terrorist Organization," U.S. Department of State Archive, Sept. 10, 2001.

62. National Security Archive, The George Washington University, accessed Nov. 9, 2024, https://nsarchive2.gwu.edu/NSAEBB/NSAEBB131/dia910923.pdf.

63. National Security Archive, The George Washington University, accessed Nov. 9, 2024, https://nsarchive2.gwu.edu/NSAEBB/NSAEBB131/dia910923.pdf.

64. Villar and Cottle, *Cocaine, Death Squads, and the War on Terror*, 175–76.

65. Laila Abu Shihab Vergara, "Tensión y zozobra en la cuna del Clan del Golfo," *Vorágine*, Apr. 2, 2023 (translation mine).

66. Santiago Olivares Tobón, "Los homicidios en el Urabá antioqueño se incrementaron 275% en enero: ¿qué está pasando?," *El Colombiano*, Jan. 25, 2024.

67. M. A. Reclus, *Exploraciones a los istmos de Panamá y de Darién en 1876, 1877 y 1878* (Madrid, 1881), 54 (translation mine).

68. Andy Newman, Julie Turkewitz and Juan Arredondo, "Adams Went South to Deter Migrants. Many Say They'll Come Anyway," *The New York Times*, Oct. 7, 2023.

69. Patrick Reilly, "Texas Gov. Greg Abbott Pledges to Keep Bussing Migrants to NYC, Takes Shot at Mayor Eric Adams in NRA Speech," *New York Post*, May 18, 2024.

70. Victoria Eugenia Henao, *My Life with Pablo* (Ebury Press, 2019), 271.

71. Ryszard Kapuściński, *Another Day of Life* (Knopf Doubleday Publishing Group, 2001), 56.

72. Julie Turkewitz, "A Girl Loses Her Mother in the Jungle, and a Migrant Dream Dies," *The New York Times*, Nov. 9, 2022.

73. Cristopher Sherman, "The Jungle Between Colombia and Panama Becomes a Highway for Migrants from Around the World," The Associated Press, Dec. 17, 2023.

74. Manuel Mateo Pérez, "Los últimos días de Antonio Machado y la culpabilidad escondida de su hermano Manuel," *El Mundo*, Feb. 22, 2019.

75. Jessica Purkiss and Jack Serle, "Obama's Covert Drone War in Numbers: Ten Times More Strikes Than Bush," *The Bureau of Investigative Journalism*, Jan. 17, 2017.

76. Jack Serle, "Trump's 100 Days: U.S. Air Campaign Hammers Yemen with Almost a Strike a Day," *The Bureau of Investigative Journalism*, Apr. 27, 2017.

77. Maggie Michael, "Sexual Abuses Rampant in UAE-Controlled Prisons in Yemen," The Associated Press, June 21, 2018.

78. "La campaña política que se lucra con la plata que les cobra a los migrantes en el Darién," *Vorágine*, Oct. 1, 2023.

79. Joanna Apap with Sami James Harju, "The Concept of 'Climate Refugee': Towards a Possible Definition," European Parliamentary Research Service, Oct. 2023.

80. Jon Henley, "Climate Crisis Could Displace 1.2bn People by 2050, Report Warns," *The Guardian*, Sept. 9, 2020.

81. Julie Turkewitz, "Sexual Assault of Migrants in Panama Rises to Level Rarely Seen Outside War," *The New York Times*, Apr. 4, 2024.

82. Kane, *Phantom Gringo Boat*, 44.

83. Thomas L. Friedman, "Foreign Affairs Big Mac I," *The New York Times*, Dec. 8, 1996; "Thomas Friedman Can't Stop Comparing Afghanistan to a 'Special Needs Baby,'" *AlterNet*, Dec. 7, 2009; Belén

Fernández, *The Imperial Messenger: Thomas Friedman at Work* (Verso, 2011), 48; Thomas L. Friedman, "Israel's Goals in Gaza?," *The New York Times*, Jan. 13, 2009.

84. Thomas L. Friedman, "As Ugly as It Gets," *The New York Times*, May 25, 2010.

85. Tatiana Escárraga, "San Andrés, un paraíso bajo el violento control del Clan del Golfo," La Liga Contra el Silencio, July 7, 2022.

86. Marco Rubio (@SenMarcoRubio), X, June 17, 2024, https://x.com/SenMarcoRubio/status/1802734204096024927.

87. Alexander Cockburn and Jeffrey St. Clair, *Whiteout: The CIA, Drugs and the Press* (Verso, 1999), 167.

88. Julie Turkewitz, "Sexual Assault of Migrants in Panama Rises to Level Rarely Seen Outside War," *The New York Times*, Apr. 4, 2024.

89. "Mexico's New National Guard is Breaking its Vow to Respect Human Rights," Amnesty International, Nov. 8, 2020.

90. "CBP One™ Mobile Application," U.S. Customs and Border Protection, accessed Nov. 11, 2024, https://www.cbp.gov/about/mobile-apps-directory/cbpone.

91. Kate Rogers, "Immigrant Workers Are Helping Boost the U.S. Labor Market," *CNBC*, May 3, 2024.

92. "Discurso de toma de posesión del presidente de la República, José Raúl Mulino," July 1, 2024, https://www.presidencia.gob.pa/publicacion/discurso-de-toma-de-posesion-del-presidente-de-la-republica-jose-raul-mulino.

93. Alma Solís, "Panama President Says Repatriation of Migrants Crossing the Darien Gap Will Be Voluntary," The Associated Press, July 18, 2024.

Further Reading

Balf, Todd. *The Darkest Jungle: The True Story of the Darién Expedition and America's Ill-Fated Race to Connect the Seas*. New York: Crown Publishing Group, 2003.

Cockburn, Alexander, and Jeffrey St. Clair. *Whiteout: The CIA, Drugs and the Press*. New York: Verso Books, 1999.

Kane, Stephanie. *The Phantom Gringo Boat: Shamanic Discourse and Development in Panama*. Washington, DC: Smithsonian Books, 1994.

McCullough, David. *The Path Between the Seas: The Creation of the Panama Canal, 1870–1914*. New York: Simon & Schuster, 1978.

Miller, Todd. *Empire of Borders: The Expansion of the U.S. Border around the World*. New York: Verso Books, 2019.

Villar, Oliver, and Drew Cottle. *Cocaine, Death Squads, and the War on Terror: U.S. Imperialism and Class Struggle in Colombia*. New York: Monthly Review Press, 2011.

Walia, Harsha. *Border and Rule: Global Migration, Capitalism, and the Rise of Racist Nationalism*. Chicago: Haymarket Books, 2021.

Washington, John. *The Dispossessed: A Story of Asylum and the U.S.-Mexican Border and Beyond*. New York: Verso Books, 2020.

Weeks, John, and Phil Gunson. *Panama: Made in the USA*. Rugby, UK: Practical Action Publishing, 1990.

About the Author

BELÉN FERNÁNDEZ is an opinion columnist for *Al Jazeera*. Born in Washington, D.C., in 1982, she attended Columbia University and then got the hell out of the United States. She has now spent more than twenty years avoiding the homeland whenever possible and can often be found in Mexico, Turkey, Italy, or Lebanon. Belén is the author of several books, including *Exile: Rejecting America and Finding the World*; *Inside Siglo XXI: Locked Up in Mexico's Largest Immigration Detention Center*; *The Imperial Messenger: Thomas Friedman at Work*; *Checkpoint Zipolite: Quarantine in a Small Place*; and *Martyrs Never Die: Travels through South Lebanon*, a hitch-hiking travelogue. Acclaimed novelist Francisco Goldman has praised her work as "incredibly funny, observant, humane, anarchic, politically incisive, sophisticated, and raffish," contending that "Belén Fernández is a dangerously enchanting siren."